T0180967

Contributions to Statistics

For further volumes:
http://www.springer.com/series/2912

Niccolò Grieco • Maurizio Marzegalli •
Anna Maria Paganoni
Editors

New Diagnostic, Therapeutic and Organizational Strategies for Acute Coronary Syndromes Patients

 Springer

Physica-Verlag
A Springer Company

Editors
Niccolò Grieco
Intensive Cardiac Care Unit &
  Prehospital Emergency Care
Niguarda Hospital
Milan
Italy

Maurizio Marzegalli
Department of Cardiology
AO San Carlo Borromeo
Milan
Italy

Anna Maria Paganoni
Department of Mathematics
Politecnico di Milano
Milan
Italy

ISSN 1431-1968
ISBN 978-88-470-5625-1   ISBN 978-88-470-5379-3 (eBook)
DOI 10.1007/978-88-470-5379-3
Springer Milan Heidelberg New York Dordrecht London

Jointly published with Physica-Verlag Heidelberg, Germany

© Springer-Verlag Italia 2013
Softcover re-print of the Hardcover 1st edition 2013
This work is subject to copyright. All rights are reserved by the Publisher, whether the whole or part of the material is concerned, specifically the rights of translation, reprinting, reuse of illustrations, recitation, broadcasting, reproduction on microfilms or in any other physical way, and transmission or information storage and retrieval, electronic adaptation, computer software, or by similar or dissimilar methodology now known or hereafter developed. Exempted from this legal reservation are brief excerpts in connection with reviews or scholarly analysis or material supplied specifically for the purpose of being entered and executed on a computer system, for exclusive use by the purchaser of the work. Duplication of this publication or parts thereof is permitted only under the provisions of the Copyright Law of the Publisher's location, in its current version, and permission for use must always be obtained from Springer. Permissions for use may be obtained through RightsLink at the Copyright Clearance Center. Violations are liable to prosecution under the respective Copyright Law.
The use of general descriptive names, registered names, trademarks, service marks, etc. in this publication does not imply, even in the absence of a specific statement, that such names are exempt from the relevant protective laws and regulations and therefore free for general use.
While the advice and information in this book are believed to be true and accurate at the date of publication, neither the authors nor the editors nor the publisher can accept any legal responsibility for any errors or omissions that may be made. The publisher makes no warranty, express or implied, with respect to the material contained herein.

Printed on acid-free paper

Physica is a brand of Springer
Springer is part of Springer Science+Business Media (www.springer.com)

Preface

The contributions published in this volume are the result of a selection based on the presentations given at the Workshop on "Identification and development of new diagnostic, therapeutic, and organizational strategies for patients with Acute Coronary Syndromes" held in Milan on February 15, 2012.

The workshop was a conclusive event of a 3-year-long strategic program supported by Italian Ministry of Health and Health Governance of Regione Lombardia.[1]

Objective of the strategic program was the identification of new diagnostic, therapeutic, and organizational strategies to be applied to patients with Acute Coronary Syndromes (ACS), in order to improve the occurrence of clinical outcomes.

Patients with ACS are at high risk of thrombosis (acute ischemic events), arrhythmias (sudden death due to ventricular fibrillation), and a variety of complications due to the complexity of therapeutic intervention (hemorrhagic disorders, contrast-induced nephropathies, thrombosis of coronary stents).

The first part of Strategic Program was structured in two functional subparts: the first one was the statistical design of a region-wide registry automatically linked with administrative Public Health Database. The Registry is still ongoing; periodical statistical analysis was performed with innovative methods to deal with complex large databases. At the same time a subproject analyzed the best pattern to use existing administrative databases to clinical and epidemiological purposes.

The second part of Strategic Program was divided in three subprojects which take advantage on new biomolecular and imaging strategies aimed at the identification of patients with ACS at the highest risk of:

- Thrombotic complications due to reduced renal function and prothrombotic activation of blood elements.
- Ventricular fibrillation and sudden death after acute myocardial infarction, due to the prevalence of genetic polymorphisms relevant for the disease.

- Poor revascularization consequent to reduced ventricular viability or function as identified with new imaging techniques, also in relation to newly identified biomarkers.

Also this volume is structured in two different parts: first one focused on cooperative project mainly on statistical analysis of large clinical and administrative databases; second one focused on the development of innovative diagnostic techniques for the precocious identification of patients at major risk.

We wish to thank all referees for their valuable contributions that made this volume possible and Maurizio Bersani, Gabriella Borghi, Luciano Bresciani, Massimo Casciello, Elena Corrada, Giancarlo Fontana, Carlo Lucchina, Maria Novello Luciani, Antonio Mafrici, Silvio Marenzi, Antonio Marzocchi, Lorenzo Menicanti, Luca Merlino, Luigi Oltrona Visconti, Peter J. Schwartz, Giovanni Sesana, Caterina Tridico, and Carlo Zocchetti.

Milan, Italy   Niccolò Grieco
January 2013   Maurizio Marzegalli
                                                                                   Anna Maria Paganoni

---

[1] "Development of new diagnostic, therapeutic and organizational strategies to be applied to patients with Acute Coronary Syndromes" with five Project parts (Programma Strategico Ricerca Finalizzata Ministero della Salute (Anno 2007) "Sviluppo di nuove strategie conoscitive, diagnostiche, terapeutiche e organizzative in pazienti con sindromi coronariche acute" (ex art. 12 D.Lgs. n. 502/1992)):

- Project part of Strategic Program 1—RFPS-2007-2-634753
  Institution presenting the project: Regione Lombardia—Direzione Generale Sanità
  "Exploitation, integration and study of current and future health databases in Lombardia for Acute Myocardial Infarction"
  Scientific Coordinator: Marzegalli Maurizio
- Project part of Strategic Program 2—RFPS-2007-2-634780
  Institution presenting the project: Centro Cardiologico Monzino, IRCCS
  "Identification of proteomic/proinflammatory and immune biomarkers in patients with Acute Coronary Syndromes at high risk to develop clinical events: genomic and proteomic approaches"
  Scientific Coordinator: Marenzi Gian Carlo Silvio
- Project part of Strategic Program 3—RFPS-2007-2-644418
  Institution presenting the project: Istituto Auxologico Italiano
  "Ventricular fibrillation during myocardial infarction: genetic basis"
  Scientific Coordinator: Schwartz Peter J.
- Project part of Strategic Program 4—RFPS-2007-2-634791
  Institution presenting the project: Regione Emilia-Romagna
  "Detection, characterization and prevention of Major Adverse Cardiac Events after Drug Eluting Stent implantation in patients with Acute Coronary Syndrome"
  Scientific Coordinator: Marzocchi Antonio
- Project part of Strategic Program 5—RFPS-2007-2-644709
  Institution presenting the project: IRCCS Policlinico San Donato
  "Pathogenesis and therapy of acute myocardial infarction: new perspectives and innovative therapeutic strategies"
  Scientific Coordinator: Menicanti Lorenzo

Contents

Part I
Organizational Strategies in ACS

Gender Differences in Hospitalization for Acute Myocardial Infarction in Lombardy During the Years 2000–2010

Elena Corrada, Cristina Mazzali, Pietro Barbieri, Giuseppe Ferrante, Maurizio Marzegalli, Marco Mennuni, Luca Merlino, Patrizia Presbitero, and Piera Angelica Merlini

Abstract The industrialized world is undergoing epidemiologic variations in acute coronary syndrome and the female gender is particularly involved in these changes. Our study was designed based on administrative databases of all hospital admissions in the Lombardy region during the years 2000–2010 which enabled us to obtain complete and updated information regarding the gender-related epidemiologic situation.

Women present an incidence and attack rate of acute myocardial infarction which is approximately half that of men, but this difference is influenced by age, type of infarction, and the period of time examined. The female population with acute myocardial infarction is generally 10 years older than the male population (mean age 76 vs. 66 years), and above 75 years of age the number of infarctions in women exceeds that in males, even though incidence is still higher in the male

E. Corrada (✉) • C. Mazzali • G. Ferrante • M. Mennuni • P. Presbitero
Department of Cardiology, Humanitas Clinical and Research Center, Rozzano, Milan, Italy
e-mail: elena.corrada@humanitas.it; cristina.mazzali@unimi.it;
giuseppe.ferrante@humanitas.it; marco.mennuni@gmail.com;
Patrizia.presbitero@humanitas.it

P. Barbieri
Department of Cardiology, Ospedale Uboldo, Cernusco sul Naviglio, Milan, Italy
e-mail: pietro.barbieri@fastwebnet.it

M. Marzegalli
Department of Cardiology, AO San Carlo Borromeo, Milan, Italy
e-mail: marzegalli@tin.it

L. Merlino
Government Unit of the Local Health Service and Policies of Appropriateness and Control,
Regione Lombardia, Milan, Italy
e-mail: Luca_Merlino@regione.lombardia.it

P.A. Merlini
Department of Clinical Research and Cardiovascular Genetics, Azienda Ospedaliera Niguarda
Cà Granda, Milan, Italy
e-mail: Piera.Merlini@OspedaleNiguarda.it

N. Grieco et al. (eds.), *New Diagnostic, Therapeutic and Organizational Strategies for Acute Coronary Syndromes Patients*, Contributions to Statistics,
DOI 10.1007/978-88-470-5379-3_1, © Springer-Verlag Italia 2013

gender. ST elevation myocardial infarction is the most frequent type of infarction for both sexes, but non-ST elevation myocardial infarction is more frequent in women than in men, and unspecified myocardial infarction is similar in both sexes. Overall incidence and attack rate of acute myocardial infarction have dropped in both sexes over the last few years; this reduction is mainly supported by the decrease in ST elevation myocardial infarction in males. Non-ST elevation myocardial infarction significantly increases even threefold, in the same way for both sexes, after the introduction of troponin. Unspecified MI is similar in both genders and decreases over the years to reach very low numbers.

Even though lower in number, the incidence of acute myocardial infarction in females is not insignificant and, contrary to popular belief, must be considered a health problem in women as well as men. Diagnostic–therapeutic protocols during acute myocardial infarction must take into account the wide range of elderly women who suffer infarction and are not usually included in randomized clinical trials. Health organizations must be equipped to handle ever increasing aging populations consisting of frail patients with comorbidities and social–family problems.

1 Introduction

It is known that incidence of acute myocardial infarction (MI) has twice the incidence in men than in women, and this difference changes according to age influencing women particularly after menopause [1–7].

Modifications in epidemiology of acute coronary syndrome (ACS) have occurred in the western world due to older age of the general population, greater prevention and treatment strategies of cardiovascular risk factors, and earlier and more aggressive treatment of ACS. The incidence of acute MI has diminished over the years [1, 8–14], but considering the increase in incidence of AMI with age and the increase in average life expectation, the absolute number of acute MI that we observe and treat is increasing. The clinical presentation of ACS has changed following a drop in incidence of ST elevation myocardial infarction (STEMI) in respect to that of non-ST elevation myocardial infarction (NSTEMI) [2, 4, 8–10, 15–17] which is more frequent in women and the elderly [3–5, 18]. These changes could primarily affect the female gender which notoriously presents a longer average life expectation and is approximately 10 years older than males on presentation of acute MI.

The MONICA project [19], together with other studies and national registries, has illustrated the incidence of infarction in the two genders between the 1980s and 1990s. These sources of information [1] are not however updated to recent years where the above-mentioned epidemiologic variations are taking place, they only concern test areas, and the MONICA diagnostic criteria used are different from the latest international acute MI definitions [20], and exclude persons >75 years who conversely make up a high percentage of our patients.

Recent years have seen development in the use of administrative databases made up of hospital discharge records (HDR) as an updated and not selected source of information regarding all admissions and all local health centers, and the validity and correct usage of this source has been demonstrated [21–25]. Many of these studies however have been carried out on populations with ethnic characteristics which differ from those of Italian populations (USA and Northern Europe).

The Lombardy region offers an interesting epidemiologic observatory, thanks to the large population (about ten million inhabitants), to the presence of a local hospital network with modern healthcare facilities and an updated and controlled administrative database of HDR.

Our aim is to calculate and compare the two genders for overall incidence and attack rate of acute myocardial infarction and the various nosological entities and to evaluate their temporal trend in the years 2000–2010.

2 Methods

The cohort of patients that make up our study population was extracted from the regional HDR database relating to admissions (regional and extra-regional) of residents in the Lombardy region during the years 2000–2010.

The algorithm for extracting cases refers to data published in the literature [21] and is briefly described herein. We extracted all the HDRs from admission archives which, based on the main diagnosis on discharge, belonged to major diagnostic category (MDC) groups 1, 4, and 5 corresponding to diseases of the neurologic, respiratory, and cardiocirculatory apparatus. From this first extraction, all hospital admissions for infarction were identified according to the following criteria: all admissions of patients aged >18 years, with codes from 410.00 to 410.91 (ICD-9-CM code) in primary or secondary diagnosis if in primary diagnosis, major cardiac complication identification codes were used (4271, 42741, 42742, 4275, 4281, 4295, 4296, 42971, 42979, 42981, 5184, 7802, 78551, 41410, 4230). All admissions with a hospital stay of ≤ 1 day without death or transferral to another facility as reason for discharge were excluded. An anonymous code was generated for each patient in order to identify all admissions relating to the same person and in order to create a link with the regional personal data register. All cases for which it was not possible to identify an assisted code of unique link with personal database were excluded.

Two hospital admissions of the same patient were considered related to a single infarction episode if these were separated by no more than 1 day. All infarction episodes separated by at least 28 days were considered single events.

Infarction was defined according to the codes of ICD-9-CM classification that considered STEMI when the code was 410.0–410.6 (definition = acute myocardial infarction with ST elevation), NSTEMI when code was 410.7 (definition = subendocardial infarction without ST elevation), and unspecified site MI when code was 410.8–410.9 (definition = acute myocardial infarction of other specified site and acute myocardial infarction of unspecified site). The definition of STEMI and NSTEMI is based on current guidelines [20]; unspecified site MI is used if ECG's feature doesn't allow a classification. An episode was classified as STEMI when at least one of the hospital admissions comprised therein was classified as STEMI; it was classified as NSTEMI if there were no STEMI admissions and as unspecified MI if there were no admissions for STEMI or NSTEMI.

Data referring to sex, age, and date of admission were extracted from the HDR.

The number of new infarction events admitted over the survey period was defined as incidence rate of infarction of the whole resident population (expressed as number of new events every 100,000 residents). Infarction events without prior events occurring within at least 5 years were considered new incident events and for this analysis data from the years 1995–1999 were used as historic reference and the incidence was calculated for the period 2000–2010.

The number of infarction events admitted during the survey period was considered as attack rate on the overall resident population (expressed as number of events every 100,000 residents).

The incidence rate and attack rate are expressed as crude rate and standardized rate. Rates were calculated using the ISTAT [26] data of the population resident in the Lombardy region during the years 2000–2010 for point estimate of the age. The reference population used for standardization with direct method was the European population (European Union—27 countries) at 1 January 2005 (source of data EUROSTAT) [27].

The descriptive statistics of each variable show in table form the numerosity values, mean (or frequency), standard deviation, median, and confidence interval at 95 %.

The descriptive variables and rates of incidence and attack are calculated and reported separately for the two genders in total and in the various age ranges in 10-year age intervals (18–44, 45–54, 55–64, 65–74, 75–84, and ≥85 years). Separate analyses were carried out for various types of infarction (STEMI, NSTEMI and unspecified site MI).

The analysis was carried out using the 9.2 version of the SAS statistical package.

3   Results

3.1   Study Population

ISTAT data for the Lombardy region show that in the year 2000 there were 8,971,154 residents (4,630,593 women and 4,340,561 men) which increased progressively to 9,826,141 (5,023,778 women and 4,802,363 men) in 2010.

Table 1 Distribution among the two sexes of episodes divided between the various types of infarction

Type of infarction	Total	Women	Mean ± sd age	Men	Mean ± sd age
STEMI	97,299	32,555 (33 %)	75.1 ± 12.1	64,744 (67 %)	64.1 ± 12.7
NSTEMI	64,470	24,943 (39 %)	76.8 ± 11.2	39,527 (61 %)	68.7 ± 12.5
Unidentified MI	11,146	5,348 (48 %)	81.3 ± 10.1	5,798 (52 %)	73.2 ± 12.6
Total	172,915	62,846 (36 %)	76.3 ± 11.7	110,069 (64 %)	66.2 ± 12.9

MI myocardial infarction, *NSTEMI* non-ST elevation myocardial infarction, *sd* standard deviation, *STEMI* ST elevation myocardial infarction

Table 2 Age of the population with infarction in two genders in the years 2000–2010

	Women		Men	
Year	Mean ± sd	Median	Mean ± sd	Median
2000	74.5 ± 11.6	76	64.4 ± 12.5	65
2001	75.3 ± 11.4	77	65.0 ± 12.6	65
2002	75.9 ± 11.6	78	65.6 ± 12.7	66
2003	76.5 ± 11.5	78	66.0 ± 12.8	67
2004	76.3 ± 11.6	78	65.9 ± 12.9	66
2005	76.3 ± 11.7	78	66.2 ± 13.0	67
2006	76.4 ± 11.7	79	66.6 ± 12.9	67
2007	76.6 ± 11.7	79	66.7 ± 12.8	67
2008	76.9 ± 11.6	79	67.2 ± 12.9	68
2009	76.4 ± 12.2	79	66.8 ± 12.9	68
2010	77.1 ± 11.8	80	67.1 ± 13.1	68

sd standard deviation

3.1.1 Description of the Cases with Acute Myocardial Infarction

A total of 172,915 episodes of infarction have been identified in the HDR database of hospital admissions of Lombardy residents during the years 2000–2010, and, of these, 171,131 are classified as infarction events. There were 153,813 patients with at least one episode of infarction. Thirty-six percent of the population were women.

Infarction was classified as STEMI in 97,299 (56 %) episodes, NSTEMI in 64,470 (37 %), and as unspecified site MI in 11,146 (7 %). Gender distribution of the various types of infarction shows diversities (Table 1): the percentage of women is always lower than that of men for all types of infarction but increases from 33 % in STEMI, to 39 % in NSTEMI, to 48 % in unspecified MI.

The mean age for men is 66.2 ± 12.9 and women is 76.3 ± 11.7. The mean age of the population increases for both sexes over the 10-year study period going from 64.4 ± 12.5 to 67.1 ± 13.1 in men and 74.5 ± 11.6 to 77.1 ± 11.8 in women (Table 2). Distribution for age is different in the two sexes: 20 % of male patients are less than 55 years old, compared with just 5.6 % of women, whereas 29 % of male patients are older than 75 years in respect to 63 % women. Once past 75 years old, the number of women with infarction almost reaches that of men, and over

Table 3 Age range distribution in the two genders with infarction

| | Total infarctions | | | | | |
| | Men | | Women | | Total | |
Age	No. of episodes	%	No. of episodes	%	No. of episodes	%
<45	5,576	5.1	922	1.5	6,498	3.8
45–54	16,419	14.9	2,596	4.1	19,015	11.0
55–64	26,003	23.6	6,215	9.9	32,218	18.6
65–74	30,064	27.3	13,528	21.5	43,592	25.2
75–84	24,268	22.0	23,452	37.3	47,720	27.6
>84	7,739	7.0	16,133	25.7	23,872	13.8
Total	110,069		62,846		172,915	

84 years it is higher (Table 3). The different distribution among the two genders is also influenced by the type of infarction: for STEMI patients over 75 years old, we found 22.6 % men compared with 58.4 % women, but among NSTEMI and unspecified MI, men are 36.6 % and 51.2 %, respectively, and women 65.1 % and 80.7 % (Table 4).

3.2 Infarction Incidence Rate in the Two Sexes During the Years 2000–2010

The crude incidence rate of new cases of infarction in the years 2000–2010 goes from 172 to 180 cases/year in every 100,000 residents for males, with an initial upward trend to 204 cases/year which slightly drops in the last 3 years. The incidence is slightly higher in women that half of men, with a similar trend over the years going from 82 to 114 to then drop to 101 cases/year in every 100,000 inhabitants. Crude incidence rate is higher than that standardized to the European population (Table 5) (Fig. 1).

Analysis for age of the different incidence of new cases of infarction in the two sexes (Fig. 2) demonstrates that:

- The incidence of infarction increases progressively with age in each sex going from four to five cases every 100,000 inhabitants in women below 45 years of age to more than 800 cases in those over 85 years old and from approximately 25 cases every 100,000 residents in men below 45 years of age to more than 1,000 cases in those over 85 years.
- The increase in incidence of infarction occurs progressively in different ways in the two genders during the various 10-year age ranges. Incidence increases approximately tenfold from the first age bracket (18–44) to the second (45–54) and then continues to rise in males by about 50 % for each age group, while in females it increases continually to over 100 %. Consequently the male/female

Table 4 Age range distribution of the various types of infarction in the two genders

Age	STEMI				NSTEMI				Unspecified MI			
	Men		Women		Men		Women		Men		Women	
	No. of episodes	%	No. of episodes	%	No. of episodes	%	No. of episodes	%	No. of episodes	%	No. of episodes	%
<45	4,065	6.3	608	1.9	1,382	3.5	288	1.2	129	2.2	26	0.5
45–54	11,686	18.0	1,640	5.0	4,342	11.0	863	3.5	391	6.7	93	1.7
55–64	17,197	26.6	3,720	11.4	7,987	20.2	2,247	9.0	819	14.1	248	4.6
65–74	17,208	26.6	7,558	23.2	11,368	28.8	5,302	21.3	1,488	25.7	668	12.5
75–84	11,381	17.6	11,495	35.3	11,013	27.9	9,927	39.8	1,874	32.3	2,030	38.0
>84	3,207	5.0	7,534	23.1	3,435	8.7	6,316	25.3	1,097	18.9	2,283	42.7
Total	64,744		32,555		39,527		24,943		5,798		5,348	

MI myocardial infarction, NSTEMI non-ST elevation myocardial infarction, STEMI ST elevation myocardial infarction

Table 5 Number of new incident events of infarction and crude and standardized incidence rate during the years 2000–2010 in both sexes

Year	Sex	New incident events	Total male residents	Total female residents	Crude incidence rate	95 % CI		Standardized incidence rate	95 % CI	
2000	F	3,807		4,630,593	82	80	85	77	74	79
	M	7,487	4,340,561		172	169	176	167	163	170
2001	F	4,142		4,645,746	89	86	92	82	79	84
	M	8,293	4,358,338		190	186	194	182	178	186
2002	F	4,748		4,659,197	102	99	105	91	88	93
	M	8,429	4,374,405		193	189	197	182	178	186
2003	F	4,891		4,691,386	104	101	107	91	89	94
	M	8,897	4,417,259		201	197	206	187	183	191
2004	F	5,231		4,748,842	110	107	113	96	93	99
	M	9,128	4,497,954		203	199	207	187	183	191
2005	F	5,500		4,813,100	114	111	117	99	96	101
	M	9,331	4,579,992		204	200	208	187	183	191
2006	F	5,318		4,850,461	110	107	113	93	91	96
	M	9,438	4,624,741		204	200	208	185	181	189
2007	F	5,589		4,885,089	114	111	117	96	93	98
	M	9,295	4,660,352		199	195	204	178	174	182
2008	F	5,114		4,930,919	104	101	107	85	83	88
	M	8,798	4,711,487		187	183	191	164	161	168
2009	F	5,384		4,980,306	108	105	111	88	86	91
	M	9,159	4,762,370		192	188	196	167	164	170
2010	F	5,049		5,023,778	101	98	103	80	78	83
	M	8,654	4,802,363		180	176	184	155	151	158

CI confidence interval

incidence ratio of new cases of infarction goes from approximately 5.5 times in patients under 45 years of age to 1.5 times in patients over 85 years.

- The drop in incidence of infarction over the last few years appears to generally involve the older age group of both sexes.

3.3 Infarction Attack Rate in the Two Genders During the Years 2000–2010

3.3.1 Overall Infarction Events

The number of overall events of infarction/year (Table 6) in women is always about half that of men, and it has progressively increased from 2000 to 2010 in both genders going from 7,718 to 10,496 in males and from 3,957 to 6,260 in females. The increase in number of infarction events has, however, been greater in women (58 %) than in men (36 %).

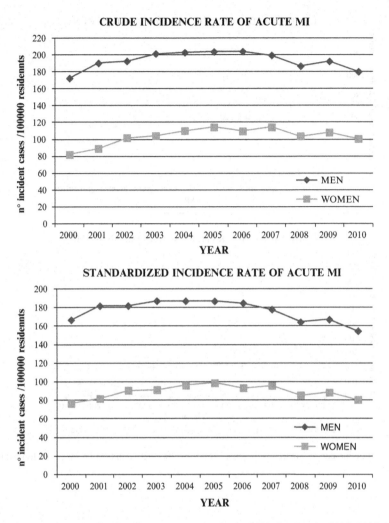

Fig. 1 Crude and standardized incidence rate trends of acute MI in Lombardy (2000–2010) in the two sexes

The overall crude attack rate (Fig. 3) went from 85 to 125 with a peak of 132 in 2007 in females and from 178 to 219 with a peak, in 2006, of 233 in males. The increase continues from 2000 to 2005 in both genders stabilizing in women and showing a slight drop in men over the last 2 years.

The attack rate (Table 6, Fig. 3) standardized to the European population is always lower than the crude rate.

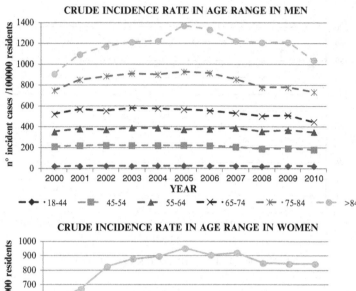

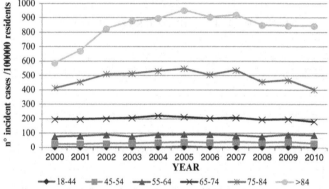

Fig. 2 Crude incidence rate trends of acute MI during 2000–2010 in the two sexes subdivided into age range

3.3.2 Analysis by Type of Infarction

The number of STEMI events (Table 7) over the last years is slightly diminishing but this is more evident in males. The attack rate of STEMI (Fig. 4) shows a progressive decrease in males, whereas for females the trend is steady with an attack rate that remains below half that of males.

In both genders the increase in overall number of infarctions (Table 7) is due mainly to an increase of NSTEMI. In 2010 the number of NSTEMI was more than triple that of 2000 with a progressive increase from 2000 to 2005 which then stabilizes. The attack rate for NSTEMI too (Fig. 5) almost triples from 2000 to 2005 in both genders to then stabilize in the following years. The difference of

Table 6 Number of infarction events and crude and standardized attack rates during 2000–2010 on the total population divided between the two sexes

Year	Sex	No. of infarct events	Total male residents	Total female residents	Crude attack rate	95 % CI		Standardized attack rate	95 % CI	
2000	F	3,957		4,630,593	85	83	88	79	77	82
	M	7,718	4,340,561		178	174	182	172	168	176
2001	F	4,452		4,645,746	96	93	99	88	85	91
	M	8,854	4,358,338		203	199	207	194	190	198
2002	F	5,174		4,659,197	111	108	114	99	96	102
	M	9,112	4,374,405		208	204	213	197	193	201
2003	F	5,401		4,691,386	115	112	118	101	98	104
	M	9,819	4,417,259		222	218	227	207	203	211
2004	F	5,865		4,748,842	124	120	127	108	105	110
	M	10,159	4,497,954		226	222	230	208	204	212
2005	F	6,238		4,813,100	130	126	133	112	109	115
	M	10,451	4,579,992		228	224	233	209	205	213
2006	F	6,128		4,850,461	126	123	130	107	105	110
	M	10,797	4,624,741		233	229	238	211	207	215
2007	F	6,450		4,885,089	132	129	135	110	107	113
	M	10,653	4,660,352		229	224	233	204	200	208
2008	F	6,272		4,930,919	127	124	130	104	102	107
	M	10,654	4,711,487		226	222	230	198	195	202
2009	F	5,964		4,980,306	120	117	123	97	95	100
	M	10,257	4,762,370		215	211	220	187	183	190
2010	F	6,260		5,023,778	125	122	128	99	97	102
	M	10,496	4,802,363		219	214	223	187	183	190

CI confidence interval

attack rates in the two sexes is minor in regard to STEMI with women slightly above half that of men.

The number of unspecified MI has diminished in both sexes (Table 7). The attack rate of unspecified site MI (Fig. 6) in the population is low with a downward trend in men but stable in women. The difference between the two genders is very small.

4 Discussion

The analysis we carried out on the Lombardy region population has shown that over the last 10 years, the attack rate, and incidence rate of new cases of acute myocardial infarction remain significantly different in the two sexes with an overall ratio of approximately 1:2 between females and males. These differences are greatly affected by the type of infarction, the age range, and temporal period (2000–2010).

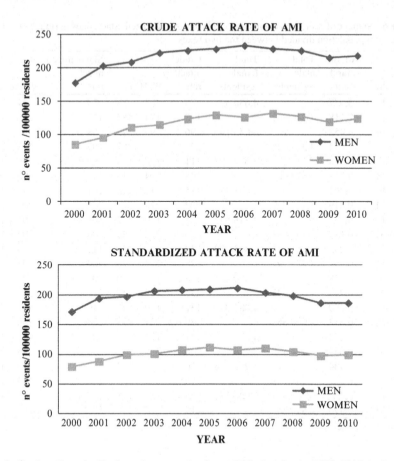

Fig. 3 Crude and standardized attack rate trends of acute MI in Lombardy (2000–2010) in the two sexes

Women with infarction in the general population are on average about 10 years older than men, with great differences according to type of infarction considered. It must be stressed that more than half of the cases in the female population is over 75 years of age and that above this age new cases of infarction are higher in women than in men as a consequence of a demographic prevalence of the female sex in the general population of that age, but the incidence still remains higher in males.

This aspect, not often noted when criteria for extracting cases pose a maximum age of 75 years [1, 11, 13, 28], is indeed relevant for diagnostic and therapeutic choices as well as for healthcare organization policies which must be carried out on the overall population affected by infarction and, in particular, on the female gender. The increase in average age of the population with infarction recorded over the last decade [4, 16] shows, in line with other countries, how our hospital organization has to manage an increasingly aging population with all the relative social and health problems.

Table 7 Number of events divided by type of infarction in the two sexes between 2000 and 2010

Year	STEMI			NSTEMI			Unidentified MI		
	F	M	TOT	F	M	TOT	F	M	TOT
2000	2,680	5,739	8,419	842	1,447	2,289	435	532	967
2001	2,826	6,116	8,942	1,202	2,208	3,410	424	530	954
2002	3,023	5,984	9,007	1,668	2,588	4,256	483	540	1,023
2003	2,966	6,111	9,077	1,947	3,117	5,064	488	591	1,079
2004	3,083	6,043	9,126	2,269	3,563	5,832	513	553	1,066
2005	3,077	5,854	8,931	2,631	4,069	6,700	530	528	1,058
2006	2,980	5,973	8,953	2,632	4,245	6,877	516	579	1,095
2007	3,166	5,917	9,083	2,774	4,257	7,031	510	479	989
2008	2,947	5,768	8,715	2,840	4,397	7,237	485	489	974
2009	2,713	5,363	8,076	2,793	4,439	7,232	458	455	913
2010	2,823	5,408	8,231	3,013	4,718	7,731	424	370	794
Total	32,281	64,277	96,558	24,612	39,046	63,658	5,268	5,647	10,915

MI myocardial infarction, *NSTEMI* non-ST elevation myocardial infarction, *STEMI* ST elevation myocardial infarction

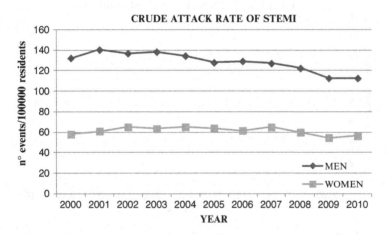

Fig. 4 Crude attack rate trends of STEMI in the two sexes

4.1 Incidence Rate

The incidence of new cases of infarction in males is approximately double that of females.

It is well known that the incidence of infarction increases progressively with age showing different progression in the two genders, connected to the hormonal and metabolic structure that in women changes significantly after menopause [3, 7, 10, 12, 28].

The incidence of infarction in women is very low before 55 years of age but progressively increases, more or less twofold every 10 years. The incidence of

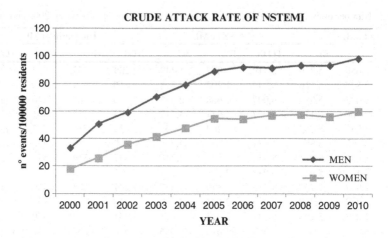

Fig. 5 Crude attack rate trends of NSTEMI in the two sexes

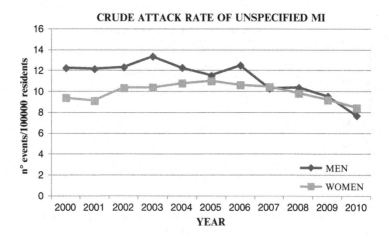

Fig. 6 Crude attack rate trends of unspecified MI in the two sexes

infarction in younger age groups is significantly higher in men than women but then the increase is progressively minor. Consequently the male/female incidence ratio of new cases of infarction goes from approximately 5:1 in patients younger than 45 years of age to 1,2:1 in the above-85-year age group.

An initial upward trend is recorded in both genders from 2000 to 2007 to then decrease in the last 3 years; the drop is more evident in men: going from 172 to 204 to then decrease to 180 cases/100,000 males and from 82 to 114 and then 101 cases/100,000 in females. The downward trend of incidence rate is also different in both genders and age groups. Indeed it appears more evident among patients over 65 years, in particular among men.

The rate of crude incidence in the Lombard population is higher than that of the standardized European population; this may be justified by the higher average age of the Italian population.

Incidence of infarction over the last 20 years has shown a downward trend [1, 8–14] due to a diffused use of coronary interventional procedures and to an increased effort to correct risk factors with the introduction of drugs with a stronger preventive cardiovascular effect such as statins and blockers of the renin–angiotensin system. Data regarding incidence of infarction reported in the literature are greatly influenced by the period of observation, the method used to identify incident cases and the population observed.

A national registry for coronary events was set up in Italy [1] in 1998–1999, where a definition was used to identify cases that comprise all coronary events (category 410–414 of ICD9) selecting just individuals under 75 years of age and excluding, therefore, a large part of the population with infarction which are especially of the female gender. Another data collection was made in Lombardy over the same period (1993–1994 and 1997–1998) using the MONICA criteria for defining cases [28]. In both studies the infarction incidence and attack rate were higher than that reported by us for both genders, but the different time period and selection criteria make it difficult to conduct reliable comparisons. Conversely, our method of collection, standardized to other experiences [21], has proven to be a valid instrument for identifying all cases of infarction presenting to hospital admission: it takes into account all episodes of acute MI of the population resident in the Lombardy region, without distinguishing between type of infarction, of hospital and without posing maximum age limits, thus offering complete information of the real world. The numerosity of the Lombard population and the accessibility to updated administrative databases, combined with the wealth of hospital resources and network organization of local emergency services, give us the possibility to extract up-to-date and reliable information regarding the incidence of myocardial infarction in Italy at the current state of treatment.

Comparing our data to those extracted with the same method from smaller populations of other Italian towns (Florence, Turin, Taranto, Rome, Pisa, Venice) during the period 2002–2004 [21], which however also comprise data relating to cases of fatal infarction not arriving to hospital and not included in our series, it is demonstrated that the standardized incidence of infarction in Lombardy is lower in men while it is similar in women. This fact could be explained if preadmission mortality were more frequent in males.

Comparison with other international series is also arduous for the reasons already stated. The series that use the MONICA criteria for selecting cases based on age (<65 or <69 years) and which are collected in a period prior to the introduction of troponin in clinical practice could underestimate cases of infarction compared to our experience, in particular for the female gender where the infarction incidence increases with age and where NSTEMI is prevalent.

Moreover, those series that also take as incident cases preadmission deaths defined as coronary could overestimate the number of infarctions compared with our data which relate to just diagnosed hospital admission cases. Moreover, the

European populations studied are those from northern countries with genetic ethnic characteristics different from those of the Italian population (Sweden, Holland, Belgium, Denmark) as well as not being homogeneous for the use of interventional procedures, drugs and lifestyles for cardiovascular prevention strategies.

In the majority of cases, the incidence of infarction, which often includes fatal prehospital cases, would appear higher for both genders than that recorded in Lombardy but with some differences.

In particular in Holland [29] during the year 2000, the rate of incidence in both sexes for just hospitalized cases was lower (189 men and 91 women) than ours maybe because of an underestimated number of infarctions compared with a more recent period coming after the introduction of troponin. In Sweden in 1985–2004 [11], using the MONICA selection criteria which only extracts cases under 65 years of age but also includes prehospital deaths, the number of infarctions is much higher than ours in the same age range in both genders. In Belgium [13], with MONICA criteria and age below 69 years, the incidence of nonfatal cases in the 2000s is higher than ours with numbers reaching 250–300 for males and about 100 for females per 100,000 inhabitants despite the lower age and therefore with a higher overall incidence. Only in the United Kingdom [30], even when taking into account prehospital deaths, the incidence of infarction in 2010 was lower than ours (130 in males and 56 in females). In the United States, during the years 2003–2005, the incidence of hospitalization for infarction appears higher than ours in both genders (approximately 350 cases/100,000 in men and 180 in women) [12].

Although there are large differences among the various populations, certain data appear constant. The incidence of infarction in both genders is different with a constant male/female ratio of approximately 2:1 and with progressive, but differing between the two sexes, incidence of infarction over the 10-year age groups a fact which brings women closer to men in the older age groups. A drop in incidence of infarction has been witnessed over the years: this is more evident when comparing the present decade to the 1990s, whereas in recent years this decrease is lower in our experience too. The drop in incidence is more evident in the male gender [11, 12].

4.2   Attack Rate: Type of Infarction and Temporal Trend

The growth of the Lombard population and its progressive aging condition the fact that the overall number of infarctions admitted to hospital every year has increased over time in both sexes.

The percentage of women on the total number of infarctions increased from 34 % in 2000 to 37 % in 2010. The American NRMI also reports an increased percentage in women from 32 to 37 %; this is more evident among patients with NSTEMI who are generally older [4].

The yearly attack rate in men is always higher than that of women, approximately 220–230 cases every 100,000 males compared to approximately 120–130 every 100,000 females, but the ratio between the two genders differs in the various types of infarction.

The overall number of infarctions in women during 2000–2010 is represented by STEMI in 52 % of cases, by NSTEMI in 40 % and by unspecified site MI in 8 %, while in men the percentage in STEMI is 59 %, NSTEMI 36 % and unspecified site MI 5 %. This diverse distribution is most certainly influenced by the fact that women are on average about 10 years older than the men. Indeed, the mean age increases in both sexes going from STEMI to NSTEMI and to unspecified MI. It is in fact well known that NSTEMI [5, 18] is more frequent in the older population and therefore in women.

A similar consideration can be made for unspecified site MI where the more difficult to collocate cases of infarction are probably classified, such as the more serious patients, those who die before being completely diagnosed, those with ECG conduction disturbances or with pacemaker stimulation.

Considering STEMI alone about 130 cases occur out of 100,000 male inhabitants, slightly twofold higher than that occurring in women (60/100,000) with a slight downward trend but only in recent years and only in males.

This may be justified by greater prevention and treatment strategies in men perhaps for age or cultural background: society considers infarction to be a male problem [31, 32].

As far as NSTEMI is concerned, over recent years 90 cases of 100,000 males and 50 cases of 100,000 females have been recorded. The attack rate for NSTEMI has increased in both genders with a slight upward trend between 2000 and 2005 to stabilize thereafter. Besides being due to the increasing age of the population, this phenomenon can also be attributed to the introduction of troponin as diagnostic criteria in clinical practice which began after the publication of the document defining infarction by the international societies in 2000 [20] with consequent extension of use of infarction diagnosis to cases previously classified as unstable angina.

The rare cases of unspecified MI have led to record an attack rate similar between the two genders (approximately 10 cases per 100,000 inhabitants in each sex). The trend in attack rate of unspecified MI in both sexes is decreasing perhaps because of an improved classification criteria applied in HDRs.

Similarities and diversities emerge when comparing our data with other experiences.

The American National Registry of Myocardial Infarction (NRMI) [4] reports that between 1990 and 2006 the percentage of NSTEMI on total infarctions increased from 14 to 59 % with an inversion in ratio between the two types of infarction events that are not observed in our experience. This may be due to an epidemiologic and therapeutic tardiness in Italy compared with the USA. Remaining in the USA, the incidence of STEMI drops for them too and is more evident in men, but higher than that observed by us, while NSTEMI increased in both sexes with temporal dynamics similar to ours [4, 9, 15, 17].

The European experiences published [6] are also difficult to compare because they cover a period of time with different criteria for data collection. In the Euro

Heart Survey carried out in cardiologic centers in the years 2000–2001 [6], where STEMI represents 58 % of infarctions, women represented only 27 % of cases of STEMI and 34 % of NSTEMI, a lower number than the 33 and 39 % in our series which also has an older mean age. The difference can be connected to the selection of participating hospitals and to a younger average age of the European population compared with that of the Lombard group (only approximately 30 % were >75 years in the European population with STEMI).

4.3   Study Limitations

The main limitation of our study is that it does not include fatal cases of acute MI not presenting to hospital. This does not allow correct confrontation with other studies in the literature. It must, however, be taken into account that in the absence of certain diagnostic criteria (ECG, myocardial necrosis marker), deaths defined as coronary represent a less defined population where a difference between the two sexes can be significant. In fact, acute MI as cause of death and sudden death is culturally more expected in males, especially in those of a younger age. Prehospital death from infarction is still an unquantifiable event that only a broader use of organized means of assistance and prehospital ECG will partially help to clarify.

   Another limitation of the study is the lack of a validation process, on the basis of the clinical documentation, in the diagnosis of different types of infarction in the administrative databases. Moreover, previous studies in the USA, Northern Europe and in Italy have demonstrated the validity and correct usage of this administrative source [21–25].

5   Conclusions

Women present an overall incidence of acute MI that is about half that of men, but this difference is influenced by the age range and type of infarction considered.

   The incidence of infarction increases with age with a diverse progression between the two sexes. The population of women with infarction is made up mainly of elderly women over 75 years of age, and, above this age, the number of women with infarction exceeds that of men. NSTEMI is more frequent in women than in men, but STEMI still remains the most frequent type of infarction for both sexes in our population. STEMI has a more evident downward trend in males, whereas NSTEMI significantly increases in both males and females after the introduction of troponin, to then stabilize. Incidence and attack rate of acute MI is lower in the Lombardy region than in many countries in both genders.

   Though numerically lower, the incidence of acute MI in the female gender is not irrelevant and, contrary to popular belief, must be considered a health problem for women too.

The prognostic therapeutic protocols for acute MI must take into account the wide range of elderly women suffering infarction who are usually excluded from randomized clinical trials [33].

Health organizations must be equipped to handle ever broader ranges of elderly populations: frail individuals, patients with comorbidities and social or family issues.

This chapter is based on research into the strategic research finalized ministerial program by the Lombardy region (RFPS-2007-3-642981): "Myocardial infarction in women: a different reality. From genetics to interventional therapy and to the psychosocial impact of the disease, first cause of death in women." Subproject of IRCCS Istituto Clinico Humanitas: "Analysis of epidemiology of AMI in the female gender from the database of Lombardy and Emilia Romagna regions."

Acknowledgments The authors wish to thank Rosalind Roberts for translating the manuscript into English.

References

1. Commissione "Epidemiologia Nazionale e Regionale": Epidemiologia nazionale e regionale. G. Ital. Cardiol. **10**, 38S–57S (2009)
2. Pilote, L., Dasgupta, K., Guru, V., et al.: A comprehensive view of sex-specific issues related to cardiovascular disease. Can. Med. Assoc. J. **176**(6), S1–S44 (2007)
3. Andreotti, F., Marchese, N.: Women and coronary disease. Heart **94**, 108–116 (2008)
4. Rogers, W.J., Frederick, P.D., Stoehr, E., et al.: Trends in presenting characteristics and hospital mortality among patients with ST elevation and non-ST elevation myocardial infarction in the National Registry of Myocardial Infarction from 1990 to 2006. Am. Heart J. **156**, 1026–1034 (2006)
5. Champney, K.P., Frederick, P.D., Bueno, H., et al.: The joint contribution of sex, age and type of myocardial infarction on hospital mortality following acute myocardial infarction. Heart **95**, 895–899 (2009)
6. Rosengren, A., Wallentin, L., Simoons, M., et al.: Clinical presentation, and outcome of acute coronary syndromes in the Euroheart acute coronary syndrome survey. Eur. Heart J. **27**, 789–795 (2006)
7. Bairey Merz, C.N., Shaw, L.J., Reis, S.E., et al.: Insights from the NHLBI-sponsored women's ischemia syndrome evaluation (WISE) study. Part II: gender differences in presentation, diagnosis, and outcome with regard to gender-based pathophysiology of atherosclerosis and macrovascular and microvascular coronary disease. J. Am. Coll. Cardiol. **47**, 21S–29S (2006)
8. Movahed, M.R., Ramaraj, R., Hashemzadeh, M., et al.: Rate of acute ST-elevation myocardial infarction in the United States from 1988 to 2004 (from the nationwide inpatient sample). Am. J. Cardiol. **104**(1), 5–8 (2009)
9. Movahed, M.R., Ramaraj, R., Hashemzadeh, M., et al.: Nationwide trends in the age adjusted prevalence of non-ST elevation myocardial infarction (NSTEMI) across various races and gender in the USA. Acute Card. Care **12**, 58–62 (2010)
10. Abildstrom, S.Z., Rasmussen, S., Rosén, M., Madsen, M.: Trends in incidence and case fatality rates of acute myocardial infarction in Denmark and Sweden. Heart **89**, 507–511 (2003)

11. Lundblad, D., Holmgren, L., Jansson, J.H., et al.: Gender differences in trends of acute myocardial infarction events: the Northern Sweden MONICA study 1985–2004. BMC Cardiovasc. Disord. **8**, 17 (2008)
12. Fang, J., Alderman, M.H., Keenan, N.L., Ayala, C.: Acute myocardial infarction hospitalization in the United States, 1979 to 2005. Am. J. Med. **123**, 259–266 (2010)
13. Coppieters, Y., Collart, P., Levêque, A.: Gender differences in acute myocardial infarction, twenty-five years registration. Int. J. Cardiol. **160**, 127–132 (2012)
14. Schmidt, M., Jacobsen, J.B., Lash, T.L., Botker, H.E., Sorensen, H.T.: 25 year trends in first time hospitalisation for acute myocardial infarction, subsequent short and long term mortality, and the prognostic impact of sex and comorbidity: a Danish nationwide cohort study. Br. Med. J. **344**, 1–12 (2012)
15. Yeh, W.E., Sidney, S., Chandra, M., et al.: Population trends in the incidence and outcomes of acute myocardial infarction. N. Engl. J. Med. **362**, 23–2155 (2010)
16. Floyd, K.J., Yarzebski, J., Spencer, F.A., Lessard, D., et al.: A 30-year perspective (1975–2005) into the changing landscape of patients hospitalized with initial acute myocardial infarction Worcester heart attack study. Circ. Cardiovasc. Qual. Outcomes **2**, 88–95 (2009)
17. McManus, D.D., Gore, J., Yarzebski, J., et al.: Recent trends in the incidence, treatment, and outcomes of patients with STEMI and NSTEMI. Am. J. Med. **124**(1), 40–47 (2011)
18. Hochman, J.S., Tamis, J.E., Thompson, T.D., et al.: Sex, clinical presentation, and outcome in patients with acute coronary syndromes. Global use of strategies to open occluded coronary arteries in acute coronary syndromes IIb investigators. N. Engl. J. Med. **341**, 226–232 (1999)
19. Tunstall-Pedoe, H., Kuulasmaa, K., Amouyel, P., Arveiler, D., et al.: Myocardial infarction and coronary deaths in the World Health Organization MONICA project. Registration procedures, event rates, and case-fatality rates in 38 populations from 21 countries in four continents. Circulation **90**, 583–612 (1994)
20. The Joint European Society of Cardiology/American College of Cardiology Committee: Myocardial infarction redefined – a consensus document of The Joint European Society of Cardiology/American College of Cardiology Committee for the redefinition of myocardial infarction. J. Am. Coll. Cardiol. **36**, 3–961 (2000)
21. Barchielli, A., Balzi, D., Bruni, A., et al.: Acute myocardial infarction incidence estimated using a standard algorithm based on electronic health data in different areas of Italy. Epidemiol. Prev. **32**(suppl 3), 30–37 (2008)
22. AHRQ (Inpatient Qualità Indicators Technical Specifications, Ver 3.2a, March 2008). http://qualityindicators.ahrq.gov/downloads/iqi/iqi_technical_specs_v32a.pdf
23. ASSR (Parte 1: Identificazione sperimentazione e validazione di alcuni indicatori di processo ed esito della qualità delle attività sanitari). http://www.assr.it/agenas_pdf/SupplMon15_Indicatori_parte1.zip
24. Castellsague, J., Stang, M.R., Tomas, L., et al.: Positive predictive value of ICD-9 codes 410 and 411 in the identification of cases of acute coronary syndromes in the Saskatchewan hospital automated database. Pharmacoepidemiol. Drug Saf. **17**(8), 842–852 (2008)
25. Austin, P.C., Daly, P.A., Tu, J.V.: A multicenter study of the coding accuracy of hospital discharge administrative data for patients admitted to cardiac care units in Ontario. Am. Heart J. **144**, 290 (2002)
26. http://demo.istat.it
27. http://epp.eurostat.ec.europa.eu/portal/page/portal/statistics
28. Ferrario, M.M., Fornari, C., Bolognesi, L., Gussoni, M.T., et al.: Recenti andamenti temporali dei tassi di infarto miocardico in nord Italia. Risultati dei registri IM MONICA e CAMUNI in Brianza: 1993–1994 versus 1997–1998. Ital. Heart J. **4**(8), 651–657 (2003)
29. Koek, H.L., De Bruin, A., Gast, A., Gevers, E., et al.: Incidence of first acute myocardial infarction in the Netherlands. Neth. J. Med. **65**(11), 434–441 (2007)
30. Smolina, K., Wright, F.L., Rayner, M., Goldacre, M.J.: Incidence and 30-day case fatality for acute myocardial infarction in England in 2010: national-linked database study. Eur. J. Public Health **11**, 1–6 (2012)

31. Lefler, L.L., Bondy, K.N.: Women's delay in seeking treatment with myocardial infarction: a meta-synthesis. J. Cardiovasc. Nurs. 9(4), 251–268 (2004)
32. Shaw, L.J., Merz, C.N.B., Pepine, C.J., et al.: Insights from the NHLBI-sponsored women's ischemia syndrome evaluation (WISE) study. Part I: gender differences in traditional and novel risk factors, symptom evaluation, and gender-optimized diagnostic strategies. J. Am. Coll. Cardiol. 47, 4S–20S (2006)
33. Lee, P.J., Alexander, K., Hammill, B.G., et al.: Representation of elderly persons and women in published randomized trials of acute coronary syndrome. J. Am. Med. Assoc. 286, 708–713 (2001)

Heart Diseases Registries Based on Healthcare Databases

Cristina Mazzali, Barbara Severgnini, Mauro Maistrello, Pietro Barbieri, and Maurizio Marzegalli

Abstract The present study aims to promote incidence and prevalence estimates, to evaluate potential benefits and harms of specific health policies and to evaluate adherence to best practice by quality indicators based on administrative and textual databases (DB).

Specific items include (a) definition of extraction criteria and data collection from healthcare DB, (b) data quality control and effective record linkage across DBs, (c) sensitivity analysis on incidence and prevalence estimates, (d) adherence to best practice by means of quality indicators, and (e) providing domain and linguistic knowledge for developing text mining tools and resources.

C. Mazzali
Department of Clinical Sciences "Luigi Sacco", University of Milan, Milan, Italy
e-mail: cristina.mazzali@unimi.it

B. Severgnini
Department of Cardiology, Ospedale Uboldo, Cernusco sul Naviglio (MI), Italy
e-mail: barbara.severgnini@aomelegnano.it

M. Maistrello
Epidemiological Research Unit, Azienda Ospedaliera Melegnano, Melegnano (MI), Italy
e-mail: magjj@yahoo.com

P. Barbieri (✉)
Quality Assessment and Risk Management, Azienda Ospedaliera Melegnano, Melegnano (MI), Italy
e-mail: pietro.barbieri@fastwebnet.it

M. Marzegalli
Department of Cardiology, AO San Carlo Borromeo, Milan, Italy
e-mail: marzegalli@tin.it

N. Grieco et al. (eds.), *New Diagnostic, Therapeutic and Organizational Strategies for Acute Coronary Syndromes Patients*, Contributions to Statistics,
DOI 10.1007/978-88-470-5379-3_2, © Springer-Verlag Italia 2013

1   Introduction

Decision makers of healthcare organizations, consumers, professional, and quality organizations need information on efficacy and costs of health services.

There is now a widespread availability of data on costs of healthcare organizations, while information on efficacy is difficult to obtain; risk-adjusted outcome measures obtained from healthcare databases are often over-interpreted, and the gap between quality measures and quality improvement may be difficult to overcome.

Randomized controlled trials (RCTs) remain the accepted "gold standard" to determine the efficacy of new drugs or medical procedures. Randomized trials alone, however, cannot provide all the information needed to evaluate the implications of particular policies affecting medical therapies. The inability to translate RCT data into practice is attributable to several factors: older patients, females, and patients with multiple comorbid conditions are underrepresented in RCTs. Furthermore, not every clinical question is amenable to RCT design. Because these limitations to the extrapolation of RCT result into actual practice, large regional databases and registries are vital to round out the needed information for quality organizations, professional societies, and consumers on the applicability of trial findings to the settings and patients of interest. Research using disease and intervention registries, outcome studies using administrative databases, and performance indicators adopted by quality improvement methods can all support decisions in order to promote the safe, effective, and appropriate use of new interventions. Monitoring trends within healthcare organizations can support effectiveness evaluations in the context of quality improvement programs.

In Italy health information systems experienced a rapid growth as a consequence of the introduction of DRGs in 1995. The development of healthcare measures for the specific aim of financing gave rise to the availability of information useful for evaluating the efficiency of the providers and the efficacy of their activities.

Health information systems in Italy are differentiated on regional basis, but they share some common features: there is a common framework corresponding to the administrative databases. Electronic textual databases are resources with growing relevance in many Italian regions. In Lombardy, a regional electronic textual information system includes discharge reports and emergency room reports of almost any hospital. This database has been built up in order to share information on individual patients for healthcare data retrieval at the individual level, but it is suitable for text mining and multipurpose evaluations at an aggregated level too.

2   Literature Review

A literature review was performed using Medline database, accessed through PubMed the free search engine from the National Library of Medicine, and was supplemented by few references relating to the Italian experience.

A search on authoritative international organization Websites (research institutions or institutional sites) was also carried out.

The main issue addressed in articulating the literature search was the identification of keywords to retrieve the most relevant references. Keywords and their combinations by means of logical operators were selected with the intent to produce a literature review focused on the following points: design and implementation of disease registries, use of administrative databases to support information in disease registries and health planning, and development of a system-oriented set of quality indicators based on current information sources; a particular focus has been placed on acute coronary syndromes.

Highlights obtained from selected references are summarized here.

2.1 Using Medical Records

A first reference in 1999 [1] describes the integration between information obtained from administrative databases with those obtained from reading medical records. An interesting point is the criteria to be used for the identification and extraction of acute myocardial infarction cases through ICD9 codes.

The study also shows that reading medical records locally, if a common method of analysis has been defined, achieves information comparable in quality to a centralized reading, apparently more rigorous.

A second interesting reference [2] describes in some detail how to estimate the "prevalence" of patients who have previously undergone hospitalization for acute myocardial infarction with a parametric analysis of survival data (Poisson model) with left truncation. The article shows that 10 years of SDO allow accurate estimates of the incidence and prevalence of acute myocardial infarction, with the exception of cases where the death occurred before arrival at hospital. Also in this study a relevant question becomes the choice of ICD9 codes for the extraction of cases.

The integrated interpretation of multiple references (two corresponding to the MONICA project [3, 4], two already mentioned [1, 2], and the Epidemiology and Prevention supplement) shows a significant heterogeneity in the criteria used to identify and extract incident cases of myocardial infarction from electronic archives.

Some references provide a methodological contribution on the utilization of electronic records in epidemiological evaluation of chronic diseases [5–7]. One of these references [5] describes a system of equations that provides a complete epidemiological description (incidence, prevalence, mortality) from a limited amount of information. This mathematical tool is the basis of a public domain software made available by the World Health Organization.

Two additional references address the use of electronic records for the purpose of health planning [8, 9]. In particular it seems possible to hypothesize a significant contribution of these archives as an information base for Health Technology Assessment [9]. Databases are classified according to the information source used and also according to their potential use to evaluate efficacy ("effectiveness"), equity, and accessibility to services. A guidance is also provided to design databases and disease registries in order to plan healthcare.

Lastly a recent editorial discusses Italian cardiac registries [10].

2.2   Quality Indicators

The "Canadian Cardiovascular Outcomes Research Team," after reviewing the scientific literature, clinical practice guidelines, and published quality measures, developed a list of quality indicators for acute myocardial infarction and evaluated their reliability, validity, feasibility, and usefulness in improving patient outcomes [11].

The "Work Group to Address the Challenges of Performance Measurement and reperfusion therapy" analyzed factors that have hindered in the United States the implementation of CMS and JCAHO indicators. The Work Group suggests some modifications: a limited number of new indicators that enhance the timing of events should be used and evidence on the quality of information sources used for the calculation of indicators (in particular the quality of clinical documentation) should be provided [12].

2.3   Use of Administrative Databases to Estimate Incidence and Prevalence

A useful reference for a comparison with our data comes from a Dutch disease registry based on SDO and mortality data, which allow to calculate prehospital mortality for acute myocardial infarction [13]. Another important study describes trends over time (twenty years) of STEMI and NSTEMI in Minnesota and shows a decreasing trend in STEMI incidence and an increase progress in NSTEMI incidence, partly due to the introduction of troponin [14].

Similar evidence, limited to NSTEMI and attributed to the introduction of troponin, emerged in an observational study conducted in the United States [15] that measured the temporal trend overall and in specific subpopulations. Two additional references can be cited since their territorial contexts in some ways are similar to ours [16, 17]. Some studies focused on ICD9-cm codes validation by adopting an approach of comparison vs. a gold standard [18–20].

2.4   Regionalization of Reperfusion Therapy

The regionalization of reperfusion therapy and the structuring of a network for the management of acute coronary syndromes have quite a long history with evidence sometimes controversial. The first interesting references are an American commentary and an Italian consensus document [21, 22].

Afterwards numerous studies addressed this issue that some evidence on the effectiveness of regionalization programs and some organizational tips have emerged. We report the most recent and interesting references [23–25].

2.5   Structuring of Networks for the Management of Acute Coronary Syndromes

Four important references were selected that describe structural and organizational factors and study their correlation with outcome [26–29]. The last of these references is an editorial addressing the issue of structuring the network in relation to the different treatment options available. None of these references contain useful elements for a formal evaluation by means of network analysis [30], all still offer important insights for comparison with other geographical areas.

2.6   Risk Adjustment and Measures of Comorbidity

Two interesting references have recently appeared on the utilization of a new index of comorbidity that incorporates the construction logic of Charlson and Elixhauser well-known indexes. This index appears to give greater weight to comorbidity [31, 32] and was used to perform some analysis in the context of this research project.

Useful suggestions were made by documents published on their websites by some health agencies or research institutes. The "Manitoba Center for Health Policy" has published a document entitled "Defining and Validating Chronic Diseases: An Administrative Data Approach" [33]. The document addresses the use of administrative database to estimate prevalence and incidence of diseases, with particular reference to chronic ischemic heart disease by means of ICD9-cm coding system.

The Agency for Healthcare Research and Quality (AHRQ) has released on its website (http://www.ahrq.gov) the document "Registries for Evaluating Patient Outcomes: A User's Guide" [34]. The paper, oriented to the assessment of outcomes, contains a set of important recommendations on the structuring of registers: the guide states that a single registry may integrate data belonging to different information sources.

A distinction is made between primary data, collected specifically for the primary purposes for which the register has been designed, and secondary data that integrate information from other sources such as medical records, administrative databases, death records, databases belonging to different institutions or professional organizations, and census data. This reference emphasizes the need to integrate information on various "existing health databases."

AHRQ is also known internationally for the development of quality indicators, in particular appropriateness and outcome indicators based on hospital discharge records (*HDR*). AHRQ indicators were adopted by Age.na.s. (National Agency for Regional Health Services) who supported the implementation of these indicators in the Italian health information system ("Gli Indicatori per la qualità: strumenti, metodi, risultati") [35].

The Joint Commission on Accreditation of Healthcare Organization (JCAHO) has proposed a set of indicators based on medical records in collaboration with professional organizations (American Heart Association and American College of Cardiology) and CMS (Centers for Medicare and Medicaid Services) [36]. This set of indicators was adopted by Age.na.s. and deals with the quality assessment of acute myocardial infarction care process.

SISMEC, the Italian Society of Medical Statistics and Clinical Epidemiology, has set up a working group on the use of electronic health records in epidemiology. The activities of this working group are related to a CCM (National Center for Prevention and Disease Control) project in collaboration with some local public health authority (ASL): "Development of surveillance systems based on the use of electronic records in public health: a pilot study in selected ASL."

3 Healthcare Databases

3.1 *Administrative Healthcare Databases*

Administrative databases play today a central role in epidemiological evaluation because of their widespread diffusion and low cost of information.

Public healthcare organizations can assist decision makers in providing information based on available electronic health records, promoting the development and the implementation of the methodological tools suitable for the analysis of administrative databases and answering questions oriented to disease management. The aim of this kind of evaluation is to estimate adherence to best practice (in the setting of evidence-based medicine) and potential benefits and harms of specific health policies.

Healthcare databases can be analyzed in order to calculate measures of quality of care; moreover, the implementation of disease and intervention registries based on administrative databases could enable decision makers to monitor the diffusion of new procedures or the effects of health policy interventions. These data reflect real-world treatment settings and unselected populations. The suitable electronic medical records for analysis are hospital discharge data, specialist ambulatory records, and drug prescription data. Specialist ambulatory file includes the medical visits and the whole diagnostic examinations performed in the emergency room setting for the patients not admitted to the hospital.

Healthcare databases in Lombardy have been used for several purposes in the field of cardiovascular diseases:

• Incidence estimates of acute myocardial infarction.
• Incidence and prevalence estimates of heart failure.
• Incidence of cardiogenic shock.

- Effectiveness evaluations for myocardial infarction and for heart failure (quality indicators).
- Survival analysis for heart failure and for ischemic heart disease.
- HTA issues: implantable cardioverter-defibrillator (ICD), transcatheter aortic valve implant (TAVI), and patent foramen ovale (PFO) closure.

Analysis of data was shared by the regulatory institution (Direzione Generale Sanità Lombardia) and professional associations (Regional heart-brain committee).

The most critical issue for observational studies using administrative databases is represented by selection criteria of the observation units: several different criteria may be used, depicting different images of prevalence or incidence of diseases, and it is mandatory to perform sensitivity analysis or validation studies on diagnoses in order to evaluate the validity of estimates.

The evidence obtained by means of administrative databases can be regarded as the first-level evidence, useful for targeting areas for which further investigation is needed; quality evaluations have to be integrated by second-level indicators (performance indicators obtained from clinical medical records) and complementary information concerning diagnostic accuracy and safety of care need extraction of data from clinical medical records and from discharge or transfer reports.

Information can be extracted by means of human work on a sample of medical records or extensive information retrieval can be performed by means of text mining techniques. Textual healthcare databases could represent in the next future a new milestone in epidemiological evaluation, allowing extraction of the information needed for the analysis of the process of care (second-level indicators, notably safety indicators), the validation of codes of the diagnoses in the administrative database, and the evaluation of the informational continuity of care.

3.2   Textual Healthcare Databases

Three purposes can be stated about information extraction from textual databases:

Quality assessment by means of quality indicators: administrative databases allow measures of mortality, volumes of procedures, appropriateness of more meaningful evaluation than this can be accomplished by means of second-level "process" indicators which can be obtained by textual electronic databases.

Adherence to guidelines can be evaluated by information extraction from medical records or discharge reports:

- Recommended pharmacological or surgical treatments for selected clinical conditions.
- Diagnostic examinations during hospital stay or in the emergency room.
- Prescribed pharmacological treatment at discharge.
- Educational documentation at discharge.
- Identification of some complications of in-hospital care by information extraction from medical records or discharge/transfer reports.

All hospitals in Lombardy adhere to "Regional Evaluation Program," which is based on the Joint Commission International (JCI) standards, notably the standards concerning clinical records and discharge/transfer reports; a common framework for this kind of documentation obviously can facilitate information retrieval by text mining tools.

The second-level indicators can be obtained by medical records according to the approach of the *Joint Commission on Accreditation of Healthcare Organizations* (JCAHO) in USA and the *Centers for Medicare and Medicaid Services.*

Validation of diagnoses: The implementation of *disease and intervention registries* based on administrative databases could enable decision makers to monitor the diffusion of new procedures or the effects of health policy interventions. Moreover this informative resource can be used for issues of health technology assessment, but the main weakness of this approach is the suboptimal diagnostic accuracy. Indeed the diagnoses are coded according to ICD9 or ICD10 coding system by means of a poor standardized procedure. "Classic" epidemiological registries are superior to registries based on administrative databases just in diagnostic accuracy; however, the information of administrative databases can be coupled with the information of textual databases in order to evaluate diagnostic accuracy and to validate diagnostic codes. Therefore, information retrieval from clinical record or discharge reports can allow diagnostic validation of discharge records and diagnostic validation of disease registries based on administrative database, coupling the power and the availability of administrative databases with the improvement of diagnostic accuracy by means of text mining.

Evaluation of continuity of care: Patients are seen by many providers in a wide variety of organizations, raising concern about fragmentation of care. There are three types of continuity: informational continuity (the use of information on past events to make current care appropriate for each individual), management continuity (a consistent and coherent approach to the management of health condition), and relational continuity (an ongoing relationship between a patient and one or more providers).

Information extraction from discharge/transfer reports can be used in order to set up indicators of informational continuity of care.

3.3 Heart Disease Registries

This chapter synthesizes data analysis about epidemiology of acute myocardial infarction and about some issues of HTA in the field of heart diseases.

3.4 Data Sources

The main source of data was the administrative database of hospital admissions of the Lombardy region. We considered hospital discharge records from 2000 to 2008 relative to MDC 1, 4, and 5. For the same patients, data on emergency services were also available and date of death was obtained from regional population registry. During the project the data were extended to include 2009 and 2010.

The duration of observation period seemed adequate to detect trend variations of incidence. Data on accesses to emergency services completed the picture of intra-hospital transfers to outline patients' clinical pathways. Time to death for all causes from the first AMI admission was evaluable thanks to death date in personal data.

Limitation to MDC 1, 4, and 5 was due to the data manager request to bound data extraction to the specific area of analysis. MDCs 1, 4, and 5 were selected after an analysis on all admission records in Lombardy region during 2006, which showed as almost all AMI cases were included in these three MDCs.

Hospital discharge data from 1995 to 1999 were processed to correctly identify incident cases of AMI; only for patients with an AMI admission between 2000 and 2008, a previous AMI admission was searched for.

Actually the lack of data on deaths for AMI occurred before hospital admission leads us to underestimate the real number of incident cases.

In order to estimate the incidence of AMI on resident population of Lombardy region, hospital admissions relative to residents occurred in other regions of Italy were added to previous data.

Other sources of data were the database of prosthesis implanted during hospital admission and the database of drug prescriptions. Only for patients with diagnosis of AMI data on specific prosthesis and drugs were collected.

3.5 Selection Criteria

In an epidemiological study, a case is considered positive for the disease of interest according to selection criteria used to detect the disease itself; selected cases could be highly different from one set of criteria to another.

A number of international agencies, equally authoritative, suggest selection criteria which lead to different estimates relative to the same condition. Examples of selection criteria for AMI proposed by various agencies are reported:

- Agency for Healthcare Research and Quality (AHRQ): 410x1 codes in principal diagnosis. Selected cases are paradigmatic AMI, to be treated according to guidelines [37].
- Agenzia dei Servizi Sanitari Regionali (ASSR): 410x0 and 410x1 codes in principal diagnosis [35].
- CCM: AMI codes in principal diagnosis or AMI codes in secondary diagnoses if cardiovascular conditions are coded in principal diagnosis. Selected cases are more heterogeneous in clinical presentation and prognosis than previous ones [38].

- MONICA-WHO: Even if different definitions exist, the most frequent requires codes from 410 to 414 in death certificate and codes 410xx or 411xx in admission data. This definition is more inclusive than others, but cases must be validated with medical record review [39].

No one definition is better than another; the researchers will choose the best definition according to the purposes of evaluation.

Access and production of information through administrative databases require shorter time than that required by a disease registry. Estimates obtained are of good quality, but a validation of diagnosis on subsamples is required.

Usually validation of diagnosis is made through the reading of medical records; however, text mining techniques could be applied to textual databases to pursue this goal. Application of this type of technique is addressed elsewhere in this book.

3.6   Data Quality

An extensive quality analysis was performed on databases and cannot be reported in detail, but a particular attention was paid to the quality of patient personal identifier.

The possibility to identify a patient with certainty is a main point in quality of administrative databases. The presence of a unique and reliable identifier allows to recognize records referred to the same patient in a single database or between databases, so that the analysis of subsequent admissions or hospital transfers would be possible. Moreover, access to outpatient care, drug prescriptions, and care pathways would be known. Eventually, a possible death date could be linked from regional population registry. The knowledge of which records were referred to the same patient was the basis for definition of "episodes of care" and "related episodes of care" (or events) as we will see afterwards.

We analyzed the quality and completeness of the personal identifier. It was present in 85.8 % of cases with a trend toward improvement over years, moving from 15.7 % to 3.0 % of absence. Absent or incorrect identifier may occur both for patients resident in Lombardy region and for nonresidents.

On the basis of previous remarks, some kinds of analysis, such as post-admission mortality or transfers between hospitals, have to be carried on using the subsample of records with a correct personal identifier. Another kind of analysis, such as in-hospital mortality, can be conducted on the entire database sample. Such difference has to be considered in reading results.

An analysis was carried on to evaluate correlation between absence of personal identifier and other variables. Cardiogenic shock, for instance, was found to be more present in records without personal identifier. Such kinds of bias have to be considered even if their effect decreases over years.

Data analysis on administrative and textual databases has been performed by traditional statistical methods and indicators (sensitivity and specificity values for validation of diagnoses using different extraction criteria, risk-adjusted quality indicators, adjusting measures by means of multiple logistic regression, survival analysis based on product-limit estimates, and Cox method), but some issues needed specific methodological tools: text mining and network analysis.

3.7 Text Mining

Text mining is a relatively recent research area and its principal aim is to fill the gap between the amount of available information and its usability. It can be defined "as a knowledge-intensive process in which a user interacts with a document collection over time by using a suite of analysis tools," to discover new knowledge and support decision-making. To this end, text mining combines methods such as information retrieval, natural language processing, machine learning, modelization by means of stochastic processes for inferential purposes, and statistical learning from data.

Text mining operations are articulated in successive stages: the identification of the collection of texts to be examined, the preprocessing of the texts of the collection that leads to the creation of an intermediate numerical dataset, the statistical analysis of this dataset, and the representation and evaluation of the results of this analysis. These stages are common to all text mining operations, but they must be adjusted in connection with the specific informational content of the texts under scrutiny and with the knowledge extraction objectives that have been set.

In recent years, much research has been devoted to the development of text mining methods and tools to be applied to biomedical texts. Biomedical literature has been mined with the aim of generating new hypothesis on the basis of the knowledge extracted. Clinical medical records have also become a target for text mining operations aimed at extracting epidemiological knowledge and at improving healthcare by supporting decision-making with the knowledge extracted.

In this context, the SISS (Sistema Informativo Socio-Sanitario; healthcare information system) promises to become a source of invaluable knowledge and an ideal target for text mining. Yet, for these potentialities to be exploited, we need to develop efficient tools and, in particular, to build lexical, terminological, and ontological resources that presently we do not have for the Italian language.

3.8 Network Analysis

Network analysis is an approach to research that is uniquely suited to describing, exploring, and understanding structural and relational aspects of health. It is both a methodological tool and a theoretical paradigm: network approaches focus on relationships between subjects rather than relationships between subject attributes (variables).

Several tools of network analysis can be adopted using the information extracted by healthcare electronic databases: patients and providers are nodes and health services are the edges of the network. The performances of the healthcare networks can be measured by means of mathematical descriptors, supporting decision makers at the organizational level by describing the "real-world" healthcare networks and providing simulation tools.

4 Incidence Estimates of Acute Myocardial Infarction

The basic observation unit is the *hospital admission* due to acute myocardial infarction. Different hospital admissions may be aggregated because they are linked by transfers from a hospital or from an emergency room of a hospital to a CCU of another hospital, usually a hospital which can perform an emergency PCI. One or more admissions linked by transfers are named *episodes of care*. Incidence is calculated on the first episode of care of the patients in the administrative database. The transfer-linked hospital admissions are identified by means of the trans-coded unique identifier of the patients. This code is available in the database but it has been trans-coded according to Italian privacy law. One or more episodes of care within a time interval less or equal to 28 days have been named as related episodes of care or *events*. These observation units have been used for a comparison with other surveys that have adopted this kind of criterion.

Table 1 depicted the incidence rate ($\times 100{,}000$) of acute myocardial infarction. These data do not include prehospital mortality because the available data allow to calculate raw mortality, not disease-specific mortality; another bias could be the wrong inclusion of patients with unobservable admission for AMI before 2000 among incident cases. This bias has been corrected by checking administrative database in the time interval 1995–1999 and excluding AMI cases before 2000. The first kind of bias will be overcome in the future because disease-specific mortality data are collected beginning from 2011.

The raw incidence is characterized by a moderate increase followed by a weak decrease. This trend may be caused by two different factors that are depicted in Fig. 1, which shows the temporal trend of the different forms of AMI.

The increase of raw incidence of AMI is attributable to a fast increase of subendocardic AMI only, probably due to the gradual introduction of troponin for the diagnosis of AMI. This phenomenon is therefore attributable only to a change in diagnostic criteria. The weak decrease in raw incidence is due to a real decrease in STEMI, as shown in other settings.

Table 1 Incidence of acute myocardial infarction (×100,000)

Year	Males	Females	Total
2000	174.1	81.9	126.5
2001	194.5	89.3	140.2
2002	199.0	103.1	149.5
2003	206.8	105.1	154.4
2004	209.2	111.0	158.7
2005	208.1	114.3	160.0
2006	209.8	111.4	159.4
2007	204.4	115.9	159.1
2008	198.1	108.1	152.0
2009	194.9	106.0	149.5

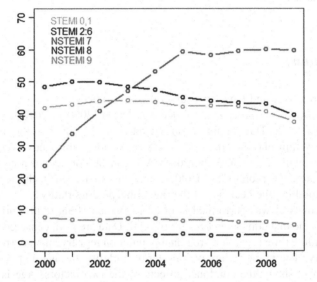

Fig. 1 The *numbers* within the *labels* represent the IVth digit of ICD9-cm codes of AMI: STEMI 0,1 anterior, anterolateral STEMI; STEMI 2–6 inferior, posterior, infero-lateral, lateral STEMI; NSTEMI 7 subendocardic AMI; NSTEMI 8 AMI NEC; NSTEMI 9 AMI NOS

5 Incidence Estimates of Cardiogenic Shock

Hospital admissions because of acute myocardial infarction and cardiogenic shock have been extracted selecting records with ICD9-cm codes 785.50, 785.51, 785.59 as secondary diagnosis and AMI codes (410.00–410.61 or 410.70–410.91) as principal diagnosis. The question is whether cardiogenic shock should be managed within the existing AMI network or whether it should be managed within a specific shock network. Case fatality rate of STEMI with shock is high (70.6 % in the first 30 days from admission, 46 % in the first day). Most of the patients (67.2 %) did not undergo to PCI or BPAC. This figure is higher in NSTEMI (88 %) with a mortality

Table 2 Raw and age-specific in-hospital mortality (%)

	2000	2001	2002	2003	2004	2005	2006	2007	2008	2009	2010
0–49	0.9	1.3	1.3	1.2	1.5	0.9	0.9	0.5	1.6	1.6	0.7
50–64	2.8	2.3	2.9	2.8	2.7	2.3	2.6	2.2	1.8	2.4	1.6
65–79	9.0	8.6	8.0	7.4	7.1	6.7	6.9	6.5	6.3	5.3	5.7
80–	20.2	19.1	18.9	17.4	17.0	17.2	17.0	17.3	16.4	16.2	15.0
Total	8.4	8.3	8.6	8.2	8.0	7.9	8.1	8.1	7.8	7.5	7.1

at 30 days of 76.6 %. These data coupled with the evidence of a low probability of PCI in high-risk patients, while RCT demonstrated the efficacy of PCI in high-risk patients, suggested to ameliorate the existing AMI network and not to organize a specific shock network.

5.1 Mortality

In-hospital mortality and long-term survival were studied.

Raw in-hospital mortality slightly decreased from 2000 to 2010, as it can be shown in Table 2. This figure is an average of the age-specific in-hospital mortalities: Within class decrease of mortality is noticeable above 65 years, in those patients with the highest mortality. Age can be considered a confounding variable because the proportion of older inpatients increased in the recent years probably smoothing the decrease of the raw in-hospital mortality.

Survival analysis was performed in order to evaluate long-term mortality. The entry point is the first admission because of AMI. Data are right censored. Information about failure time is given by regional population registry and it corresponds to raw mortality. The main factors of long-term mortality are age and comorbidity index. Figure 2 shows the combined effects of the two factors. Age is the most powerful predictor of long-term mortality. Another important factor is the ICD9-cm category of AMI. The worse prognosis is associated with residual categories (IVth digit of ICD9-cm codes 8 and 9), while subendocardic AMI exhibits a cumulative probability of survival that is between the two STEMI categories.

6 Healthcare Network

Continuity of in-hospital care for patients affected by acute coronary syndrome was evaluated on the basis of administrative data by means of network analysis. Transfers of these patients between hospitals were described and analyzed in terms of healthcare network, and their adherence to guidelines was evaluated.

We defined the healthcare network of transfers by setting hospitals as nodes. A directed link, from hospital A to hospital B, was generated if at least one patient was transferred from A to B during the year. The number of patients transferred from A

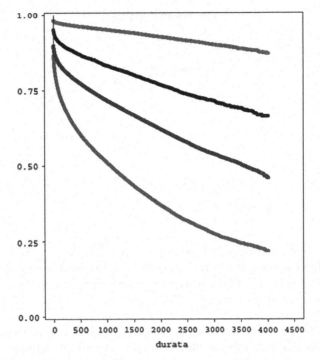

Fig. 2 Survival curves in different subsamples: age <65 low comorbidity index; age <65 high comorbidity index; age >64 low comorbidity index; age >64 high comorbidity index (descending order)

to B was the link value. Transfers from emergency room of a hospital to another hospital were also considered.

Data on transfers and hospitals were available from 2004 to 2010.

The number of hospitals, which sent or received patients, varied from a minimum of 172 in 2005 to a maximum of 198 in 2009; a tendency to increase was observed. The lowest number of observed link was 910 and was reached in year 2010; the highest was 1,074 in 2006. The mean number of total transfers over years was 6,550, standard deviation being 232.

We used Pajek 2.05© to visualize the network and to calculate principal network indices.

Network indices, e.g., centrality, may be observed over time to detect healthcare network evolution. Otherwise they may be related to clinical outcome by means of statistical analysis, as it happens for clinical variables or risk factors. Finally evolution of network may be foreseen through simulation studies as a consequence of changes or organizational interventions.

As a first result we were able to quantify the number of transfers, as well as hospitals and patients involved. An extensive analysis was carried on, but for sake of brevity, we will report only main results.

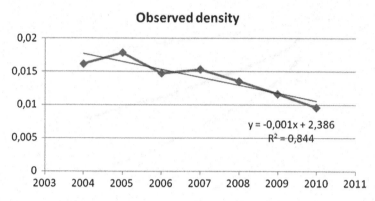

Fig. 3 Observed networks density over years

The density of a network is defined as the proportion of observed links and total number of links which could exist if all nodes in the network were linked to each other. For the observed networks, density decreased over years, and the same effect can be seen even if only transfers from acute facility to acute facility were considered (Fig. 3).

This decreasing was partly due to an increasing number of hospitals (nodes) and partly to a decreasing number of observed links. Subnetworks of transfers which ended, respectively, in bypass surgery, or in PTCA procedure, or in medical treatment were considered. Density decreasing over years was equally detected. Mean number of transferred patients received by hospitals changed from 16.6 in 2004 to 9.9 in 2010. These changes most likely reflect a reorganization of healthcare network and a better allocation of patients by territorial emergency management services.

With respect to adherence to guidelines for STEMI, a propensity for transferring young and low-risk patients (23.7 %) was observed comparing to other kinds of patients classified in terms of age and risk class (young high-risk patients 18.5 %, elder low-risk patients 14.9 %, and elder high-risk patients 6.7 %). This figure conflicts with statements of clinical guidelines. It is an example of the gap between EBM and "real-world" quality performance.

Transfers from emergency room to other hospitals were increasing over years, and propensity for transferring young and low-risk patients was also observed. Time of transfer reduced over years.

Transfers of patients with STEMI from emergency room or from acute facility were analyzed when they occurred within 24 h from patient arrival. Less than 100 transfers per year ended with a bypass surgery, and this number was constant over years; more than 800 transfers per year ended with a PTCA procedure and they too were constant over years. On the other side, the number of transfers, which ended with a medical treatment, decreased over years, with a consequent reduction of inappropriate transfers.

Fig. 4 2 STEMI transfers
within 24 h, year 2010

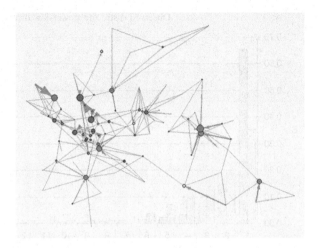

In Fig. 4 geographic distribution of transfers of STEMI within 24 h is presented. Hub centers, the biggest in the graph, are not uniformly distributed; sometimes they represent a local reference point; otherwise, in the area between Milano and Varese, the number of hub centers is considerable.

The network structure can be studied using the degree distribution, where the degree of a node is the number of links starting and/or ending in that node. In our analysis it was of particular interest to evaluate whether degree distribution fitted with "power law" distribution. In fact, a power law distribution is typical of a network strongly structured with hubs and spokes.

In Fig. 5, empirical degree distribution of observed network is compared with a "power law" distribution, whose parameters were estimated to fit empirical data. Kolmogorov-Smirnov test was applied and stated that transfers network of Lombardy region was not distributed as a "power law"; this was probably due to a high presence of reference centers.

These types of studies are still quite uncommon, and there is a lack of reference standards for healthcare networks. A comparison with characteristics of healthcare networks referred to other regions would be of particular interest, better if they were related to process or outcome indicators.

7 HTA Issues

Regional health authorities established HTA program in Lombardy since 2008. Several issues belong to cardiovascular field. Information extracted by administrative databases was used in order to answer to items about comparative effectiveness of treatments (efficacy in the real world) or to their appropriateness. The most critical issue was the correct identification of the target subpopulations by ICD9-cm codes.

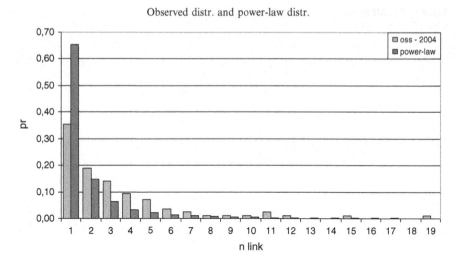

Fig. 5 Observed degree distribution and power law distribution

Efficacy of transcatheter aortic valve implant (TAVI) in selected subpopulations of patients with aortic valve disease was stated by clinical trials. TAVI performed as well or better compared to the standard treatment (AVR: aortic valve replacement) in high-risk patients. Analysis of administrative data showed that the procedure in Lombardy was performed also in subpopulations of patients with characteristics not included by clinical trials. Indeed survival analysis performed in the observational context (administrative database) showed superiority of the treatment, compared to an administrative database extracted control group, only in the subpopulations with characteristics similar to those of the clinical trials. Age was categorized in two classes (age >80 and age <81), and comorbidity was measured by a cumulative comorbidity index that takes in account all the secondary diagnoses of all the hospital admission before the index hospital admission.

No superiority of the treatment was observed in the other adult subpopulations. Therefore, the regional regulatory authorities are faced with a problem of appropriateness (Figs. 6 and 7).

The analysis of data also showed that some hospitals had a low volume of procedures. TAVI are included in the regional reimbursement program since 2008. The expected conclusion for this HTA issue is that TAVI will be kept in the regional reimbursement program only for the subpopulations of patients with characteristics which were inclusion criteria of the clinical trials (evidence of efficacy) because evidence of effectiveness was obtained in the administrative database only in these subpopulations. A regionalization program has been started for TAVI in order to avoid that patients would be treated in low-volume hospitals.

Assessment of ICD implantation and PFO closure has shown similar problems of appropriateness and existence of low-volume hospitals.

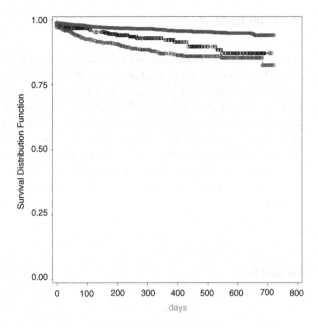

Fig. 6 Survival analysis in low-risk patients (Age <80 and combined score <1) in descending order AVR, TAVI, and control group

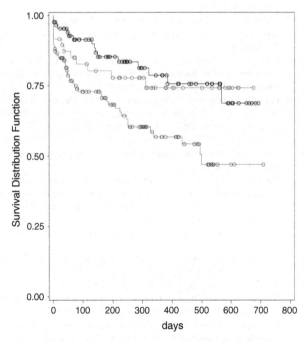

Fig. 7 Survival analysis in high-risk patients (Age >79 and combined score >0) in descending order TAVI, AVR, and control group

The conclusion is that administrative databases can support some HTA decisions whensoever a multidimensional approach is adopted, because epidemiological relevance, effectiveness (efficacy in the real world), safety, and equity of access can be evaluated by such data.

8 Conclusions

Healthcare databases can support epidemiological evaluations, quality assessment, and HTA in the setting of cardiovascular diseases. Such evaluations belong to the context of the observational studies, and therefore, they are complementary to other tools of analysis and inference about efficacy of healthcare. Healthcare databases include administrative and textual databases. Administrative databases are widespread, and informative data can be extracted to face with a wide range of problems. Textual healthcare databases are becoming widespread; information extraction and utilization need the development of specific tools of analysis, but they might represent a new important step for the development of healthcare information system.

References

1. Every, N.R., Frederick, P.D., Robinson, M., et al.: A comparison of the national registry of myocardial infarction 2 with the cooperative cardiovascular project. J. Am. Coll. Cardiol. **33**, 1886–1894 (1999)
2. Manuel, D.G., Lim, J.J., Tanuseputro, P., Stukel, T.A.: How many people have had a myocardial infarction? Prevalence estimated using historical hospital data. BMC Public Health **7**, 174 (2007)
3. Ferrario, M., Cesana, G., Vanuzzo, D., Pilotto, L., Sega, R., Chiodini, P., Giampaoli, S.: Surveillance of ischaemic heart disease: results from the Italian MONICA populations. Int. J. Epidemiol. **30**(Suppl 1), S23–S29 (2001)
4. Ferrario, M., Fornari, C., Bolognesi, L., et al.: Recenti andamenti temporali dei tassi di infarto miocardico in nord Italia. Risultati dei registri IM MONICA e CAMUNI in Brianza: 1993–1994 versus 1997–1998. Ital. Heart J. Suppl. **8**, 651–657 (2003)
5. Barendregt, J.J., Van Oortmarssen, G.J., Vos, T., Murray, C.J.: A generic model for the assessment of disease epidemiology: the computational basis of DisMod II. Popul Health Metr. **1**, 4 (2003)
6. Hanratty, R., Estacio, R.O., Dickinson, L.M., Chandramouli, V., et al.: Latino using cardio health actions to reduce risk study investigators. Testing electronic algorithms to create disease registries in a safety net system. J Health Care Poor Underserved **19**, 452–465 (2008)
7. Wiréhn, A.B.., Karlsson, H.M., Carstensen, J.M.: Estimating disease prevalence using a population-based administrative healthcare database. Scand. J. Public Health **35**, 424–431 (2007)
8. Van Brabandt, H., Camberlin, C., Vrijens, F., Parmentier, Y., et al.: More is not better in the early care of acute myocardial infarction: a prospective cohort analysis on administrative databases. Eur. Heart J. **27**, 2649–2654 (2006)
9. Raftery, J., Roderick, P., Stevens, A.: Potential use of routine databases in health technology assessment. Health Technol. Assess. **9**, 1–92 (2005)
10. Pavesi, P.C., Casella, G., Di Pasquale, G.: I registri permanenti: un sogno irrealizzabile per il cardiologo italiano? G. Ital. Cardiol. **9**, 181–184 (2008)
11. Tu, J.V., Khalid, L., Donovan, L.R., Ko, D.T., Canadian Cardiovascular Outcomes Research Team/Canadian Cardiovascular Society Acute Myocardial Infarction Quality Indicator Panel: Indicators of quality of care for patients with acute myocardial infarction. Can. Med. Assoc. J. **179**, 909–915 (2008)

12. Masoudi, F.A., Bonow, R.O., Brindis, R.G., ACC/AHA Task Force on Performance Measures, et al.: ACC/AHA 2008 statement on performance measurement and reperfusion therapy: a report of the ACC/AHA task force on performance measures. Circulation **118**, 2649–2661 (2008)
13. Koek, H.L., de Bruin, A., Gast, A., Gevers, E., et al.: Incidence of first acute myocardial infarction in the Netherlands. Neth. J. Med. **65**, 434–441 (2007)
14. Roger, V.L., Weston, S.A., Gerber, Y., Killian, J.M., et al.: Trends in incidence, severity, and outcome of hospitalized myocardial infarction. Circulation **121**, 863–869 (2010)
15. Movahed, M.R., Ramaraj, R., Hashemzadeh, M., Hashemzadeh, M.: Nationwide trends in the age adjusted prevalence of non-ST elevation myocardial infarction (NSTEMI) across various races and gender in the USA. Acute Card. Care **12**, 58–62 (2010)
16. Lambert, L., Blais, C., Hamel, D., Brown, K., et al.: Evaluation of care and surveillance of cardiovascular disease: can we trust medico-administrative hospital data? Can. J. Cardiol. **28**, 162–168 (2012)
17. Andrés, E., Cordero, A., Magán, P., Alegría, E., et al.: Long-term mortality and hospital readmission after acute myocardial infarction: an eight-year follow-up study. Rev. Esp. Cardiol. **65**, 414–420 (2012)
18. Ladouceur, M., Rahme, E., Pineau, C.A., Joseph, L.: Robustness of prevalence estimates derived from misclassified data from administrative databases. Biometrics **63**, 272–279 (2007)
19. Varas-Lorenzo, C., Castellsague, J., Stang, M.R., Tomas, L., et al.: Positive predictive value of ICD-9 codes 410 and 411 in the identification of cases of acute coronary syndromes in the Saskatchewan Hospital automated database. Pharmacoepidemiol. Drug Saf. **17**, 842–852 (2008)
20. Merry, A.H., Boer, J.M., Schouten, L.J., Feskens, E.J., et al.: Validity of coronary heart diseases and heart failure based on hospital discharge and mortality data in the Netherlands using the cardiovascular registry Maastricht cohort study. Eur. J. Epidemiol. **24**, 237–247 (2009)
21. Rathore, S.S., Epstein, A.J., Volpp, K.G., Krumholz, H.M.: Regionalization of care for acute coronary syndromes: more evidence is needed. JAMA **293**, 1383–1387 (2005)
22. di Consenso, D.: La rete interospedaliera per l'emergenza coronarica. Ital. Heart J. **6**(Suppl 6), S5–S26 (2005)
23. Singh, M., Holmes Jr., D.R., Dehmer, G.J., Lennon, R.J., et al.: Percutaneous coronary intervention at centers with and without on-site surgery: a meta-analysis. JAMA **306**, 2487–2494 (2011)
24. Patel, A.B.., Quan, H., Faris, P., Knudtson, M.L., et al.: Temporal associations of early patient transfers and mortality with the implementation of a regional myocardial infarction care model. Can. J. Cardiol. **27**, 731–738 (2011)
25. Glickman, S.W., Greiner, M.A., Lin, L., Curtis, L.H., et al.: Assessment of temporal trends in mortality with implementation of a statewide ST-segment elevation myocardial infarction (STEMI) regionalization program. Ann. Emerg. Med. **59**, 243–252 (2012)
26. Saia, F., Marrozzini, C., Ortolani, P., Palmerini, T., et al.: Optimisation of therapeutic strategies for ST-segment elevation acute myocardial infarction: the impact of a territorial network on reperfusion therapy and mortality. Heart **95**, 370–376 (2009)
27. Iwashyna, T.J., Christie, J.D., Moody, J., Kahn, J.M., Asch, D.A.: The structure of critical care transfer networks. Med. Care **47**, 787–789 (2009)
28. Huber, K., Goldstein, P., Danchin, N., Fox, K.A.: Network models for large cities: the European experience. Heart **96**, 164–169 (2010)
29. Huber, K.: Optimizing reperfusion therapy in acute ST-elevation myocardial infarction by a pharmaco-invasive treatment approach in a well-organized network. Eur. Heart J. **33**, 1184–1186 (2012)
30. Luke, D.A., Harris, J.K.: Network analysis in public health: history, methods, and applications. Annu. Rev. Public Health **28**, 69–93 (2007)

31. Gagne, J.J., Glynn, R.J., Avorn, J., Levin, R., Schneeweiss, S.: A combined comorbidity score predicted mortality in elderly patients better than existing scores. J. Clin. Epidemiol. **64**, 749–759 (2011)
32. Bottle, A., Aylin, P.: Comorbidity scores for administrative data benefited from adaptation to local coding and diagnostic practices. J. Clin. Epidemiol. **64**, 1426–1433 (2011)
33. Lix, L., Yogendran, M., Burchill, C., Metge, C., McKeen, N., Moore, D., Bond, R.: Defining and validating chronic diseases: an administrative data approach. Winnipeg, Manitoba Centre for Health Policy. http://mchp-appserv.cpe.umanitoba.ca/reference/chronic.disease.pdf (2006). Accessed 14 Oct 2012
34. Gliklich, R.E, Dreyer, N.A.: Registries for evaluating patient outcomes: a user's guide. AHRQ Publication No. 07-EHC001-1. Rockville, MD: Agency for Healthcare Research and Quality. http://effectivehealthcare.ahrq.gov/repFiles/PatOutcomes.pdf (2007). Accessed 14 Oct 2012
35. ASSR.: Gli Indicatori per la qualità: strumenti, metodi, risultati. Supplemento al n. 15 di Monitor. http://www.agenas.it/monitor_supplementi.html (2005). Accessed 14 Oct 2012
36. CMS.: The premier hospital quality incentive demonstration: clinical conditions and measures for reporting. http://www.cms.gov/Medicare/Quality-Initiatives-Patient-Assessment-Instruments/HospitalQualityInits/downloads/HospitalPremierMeasures.pdf. Accessed 14 Oct 2012
37. AHRQ.: QI, inpatient quality indicators #15, technical specifications, acute myocardial infarction (ami) mortality rate http://www.qualityindicators.ahrq.gov/Downloads/Modules/IQI/V44/TechSpecs/IQI%2015%20Acute%20Myocardial%20Infarction%20%28AMI%29%20Mortality%20Rate.pdf (2012). Accessed 14 October 2012
38. Barchielli, A.: I registri di altre patologie: solo progetti pilota, nessuna rete? L'infarto miocardico. Convegno di primavera Aie 2012 http://www.epicentro.iss.it/focus/aie/pdf2012/AIE%2028%20maggio%202012/Barchielli_AIE28mag12.pdf (2012). Accessed 14 Oct 2012
39. EUROCISS.: Indicatori raccomandati per l'Europa: Infarto acuto del miocardio. Istituto Superiore di Sanità. http://www.cuore.iss.it/eurociss/indicatori-europa/indicatori_infarto.asp (2008). Accessed 14 Oct 2012

Designing and Mining a Multicenter Observational Clinical Registry Concerning Patients with Acute Coronary Syndromes

Francesca Ieva

Abstract In this work we describe design, aims, and contents of the ST-segment Elevation Myocardial Infarction (STEMI) Archive, which is a multicenter observational clinical registry planned within the Strategic Program "Exploitation, integration and study of current and future health databases in Lombardia for Acute Myocardial Infarction." This is an observational clinical registry that collects clinical indicators, process indicators, and outcomes concerning STEMI patients admitted to any hospital of the regional district, one of the most advanced and intensive-care area in Italy. This registry is arranged to be automatically linked to the Public Health Database, the ongoing administrative datawarehouse of Regione Lombardia. Aims and perspectives of this innovative project are discussed, together with feasibility and statistical analyses which are to be performed on it, in order to monitor and evaluate the patterns of care of cardiovascular patients.

1 Introduction

Assessment of service delivery at the local level of government is not a new enterprise in clinical context, but linking the measures, or indicators, to program mission, setting performance targets, and regularly reporting on the achievement of target levels of performance are new features in the performance measurement movement sweeping across healthcare systems all over the world. A performance measure is a quantitative representation of public health activities, measured in order to evaluate, and then improve, performances and services. In fact, in order to improve something, you have to be able to change it; in order to change it, you have to be able to understand it; in order to understand it, you have to be able to measure it. In this work we present and describe the ST-segment Elevation Myocardial

F. Ieva (✉)
Dipartimento di Matematica, MOX, Politecnico di Milano, Milan, Italy
e-mail: francesca.ieva@mail.polimi.it

N. Grieco et al. (eds.), *New Diagnostic, Therapeutic and Organizational Strategies for*   47
Acute Coronary Syndromes Patients, Contributions to Statistics,
DOI 10.1007/978-88-470-5379-3_3, © Springer-Verlag Italia 2013

Infarction (STEMI) Archive, a multicenter observational clinical registry planned within the Strategic Program "Exploitation, integration and study of current and future health databases in Lombardia for Acute Myocardial Infarction" and funded by Italian Ministry of Health and by the regional district for healthcare, namely, the "Direzione Generale Sanità—Regione Lombardia." The main goal of this program is to enhance the integration of different sources of health information in order to automate and streamline clinicians' workflow, so that data collected once can be used multiple times for different aims, and especially for measuring performances of healthcare systems, to understand how hospitals work and to increase efficacy of healthcare offer in terms of costs and patterns of care. In fact, integrated systems enable people in charge with healthcare government to obtain data for billing or performance evaluations, as well as they allow clinicians to see trends in the effectiveness of treatments or to compare patterns of care. Finally, they let researchers to analyze the efficacy and efficiency of system on patients' outcomes. In other words, integrated systems play a fundamental role in complex clinical environments.

The STEMI Archive consists of clinical information collection related to patients admitted in all hospitals of Regione Lombardia with STEMI diagnosis. As in classical clinical surveys, also clinical data of the STEMI Archive are collected in order to identify subpopulations (in our case patients affected by STEMI). On the other hand, the innovative contents of this survey are represented by process indicators recorded in it: the main idea is to evaluate treatment times with the aim of designing a preferential therapeutic path to reperfusion in STEMI patients and to direct the patient flow through different pathways according, for example, to on hours vs. off hours of working timetable or to clinical conditions such severity of infarction. In this sense, this survey represents an instrument both for epidemiological enquiries and for organizational optimization of the cardiological healthcare networks. Moreover, personal data are collected so that the patient can be univocally identified also within administrative datawarehouse, and a longitudinal electronic record containing his/her previous clinical history and follow-up can be traced, thanks to the potential of Electronic Health Record (Fascicolo Sanitario Elettronico). The link between the two databases will generate the primary platform for the study of impact and care of STEMI on the whole territory of Regione Lombardia. Finally, information concerning outcomes (i.e., if a subject is discharged alive or not, if the reperfusive procedure has been effective or not) are recorded, so that they can be returned to clinicians and institutions appropriately exploited in terms of patient's case mix and care pattern, in order to support healthcare decisions and clinical policies through monitoring and analyzing data. This latter step may be carried out through suitable statistical monitoring and modeling. Statistical models, in fact, are able to capture complexity, variability, and grouped nature of these data, as we will see in Sect. 6, providing an evidence-based decisional support as well as pursuing the optimization of healthcare offer.

The STEMI Archive should overcome the difficulties faced in previous pilot data collections (i.e., $MOMI^2$, GestIMA, LombardIMA; see [1, 2]) related to nonuniformity, inaccuracy of filling, and data redundancy. In particular nonuniformity of data collection among different structures, or among successive surveys, and inaccuracy in filling dataset fields will cease to be a problem because the Archive procedure for collecting data has become mandatory for all hospitals through a directive issued by the lawmaker [3]. All centers will fill in the registry along the same protocol and with the same software, thanks to the help of Lombardia Informatica (http://www.lispa.it), the Information and Communication Technology (ICT) society which Regione Lombardia leans on for implementation of Electronic Health Record. Opinion leaders and scientific societies of cardiology agreed upon all fields to be recorded, and a unique data collector was identified in the Governance Agency for Health, which is also the data owner. Moreover, since this registry is designed to be automatically linked with administrative databases, inaccuracy of information will be partially overcome by the fact that, after the linkage, all information contained in it will be checked for coherence with those contained in Public Health Databases (PHD). Then only the information of interest will be extracted, avoiding redundance and achieving greater accuracy and reliability (for further details on record linkage, see [4]).

In the following we describe the health policy and program of Regione Lombardia concerning cardiovascular diseases (Sect. 2); then we move (Sect. 3) to an in-depth examination of the STEMI Archive and of the administrative datawarehouse of Regione Lombardia (Sect. 4), i.e., the Public Health Database (PHD). Details and aims of integration between the considered clinical registry and administrative databanks are described in Sect. 5, whereas in Sect. 6 the role of statistician and statistical analyses is discussed. Finally, conclusions and open problems are presented in Sect. 7.

2 Cardiovascular Disease and Health Policy in Regione Lombardia

The pathology we are interested in is a particular type of acute myocardial infarction, namely, ST-segment Elevation Myocardial Infarction (STEMI). It belongs to the wider class of acute coronary syndromes (ACS), and it is caused by an occlusion of a coronary artery, which causes an ischemia (a restriction in blood supply) and an oxygen shortage. These effects, if left untreated for long, can damage the heart muscle tissue (myocardium) since the interruption of blood supply to the cells makes them die (infarction). STEMI, whose incidence and mortality are very high in Italy as well as all over the world, can be diagnosed by observing abnormal elevation of ST-segment in the ECG curve. An early reperfusion therapy is one of the most important goals that must be achieved in the treatment of STEMI patients and can be obtained through thrombolysis and/or percutaneous transluminal coronary angioplasty (PTCA). The former one consists in a pharmacological treatment which causes a breakdown of the blood clots which obstruct the coronary vessel, while in the latter one, an empty and collapsed balloon on a guide wire, known as *balloon* catheter, is passed into the narrowed or obstructed vessels and then inflated to a fixed size. This allows the vessel to be opened up and the blood flow to be improved; then balloon is collapsed and withdrawn.

The strategy of the connecting net between territory and hospitals, made by a centralized coordination of the emergency resources, gives the possibility to optimize therapeutic choices and so to reduce the intervention time. The timeliness of reperfusion therapy is of central importance, because the benefits of therapy decrease rapidly with delays in treatment. Thus, American Heart Association and American College of Cardiology (ACC/AHA) guidelines recommend that thrombolysis should be provided within 30 min of first medical system contact and that primary PTCA within 90 min of first medical system contact for patients presenting with STEMI (see [5–8]).

Regione Lombardia is very sensitive to cardiovascular topics, as proved by the huge amount of social and scientific enterprises concerning these syndromes which have been carried out during the past years (see [1, 9]). With STEMI Archive and Strategic Program, people in charge with healthcare governance intended to adopt new clinical instruments and already existing administrative resources to create new methods for targeting and measuring performances in cardiovascular healthcare. In particular, *Decreto 10446* [3] establishes which are the treatment times to be measured in order to judge the hospitals quality of care service and choose the STEMI Archive as main tool for collecting, analyzing, and evaluating the goals achieved by individual hospitals. So STEMI Archive data collection has become a standardized and compulsory procedure for all hospitals in Regione Lombardia, since January 2011.

3   The STEMI Archive

In this section we describe aims and contents of the STEMI Archive. The Archive is a multicenter observational prospective clinical study, designed during the first phase of Strategic Program, i.e., during 2010, thanks to a collaboration among clinicians, people in charge with healthcare governance of Regione Lombardia, and statisticians of Politecnico di Milano. Filling the STEMI Archive is mandatory by law [3]. Three data collections have been planned within the end of Strategic Program (December 2011). The first one has already been performed during the time slot January–December 2010, to set, test and calibrate the mechanism of data collection. This testing period was needed to enable all the clinical structures involved into the project to overcome software and technical hitches and to be provided by technical assistance, especially concerning issues related to the SISS system (the Italian platform for supporting Electronic Health Record, see http://www.siss.regione.lombardia.it/). The second collection period, from January 2011 to the end of June 2011, was the first official period of data collection. Finally, a third collection period has been planned for October–December 2011. I what follows, we will present some results of a feasibility analysis of integration between data arising from the first collection previously mentioned and data from an administrative database.

The STEMI Archive, as well as every survey on specific disease, enables researchers to point out a subpopulation of interest for clinical and scientific inquiries. Starting from these subpopulations, studies on effectiveness of different patterns of care and then provider profiling can be carried on, adopting models for explaining outcomes by means of suitable process indicators and adjusting for different case mix. In our case, a primary outcome measure is incidence of MACE defined as any one of the following events: in-hospital mortality, acute myocardial reinfarction, cardiogenic shock, stroke, long-term mortality, and major bleeding. A secondary outcome measure is reperfusion effectiveness measured quantifying the reduction of ST-segment elevation 1 h after the treatment: if the reduction is larger than 50 % in the case of thrombolysis and 70 % in the case of angioplasty, we could consider the procedure effective. Process indicators and patient covariates can be resumed in the following four categories:

- *Demographic data*: *Codice Fiscale* (the alphanumeric identity code used to identify people who have fiscal residence on Italian territory), date of birth, sex, weight, height, and hospital of admission.
- *Pre-hospital data*: Diabetes, smoking, high blood pressure, high cholesterol level, and history of cardiac pathology.
- *Admission data*: Time and type of symptoms onset, time of first medical contact, time to call for rescue, type of rescue unit sent (advanced or basic rescue unit, that is, with or without pre-hospital 12d ECG teletransmission), time of first ECG, site of infarction on ECG, mode of hospital admittance, fast-track activation, Killip class (which quantify in four categories the severity of infarction), blood pressure, cardiac frequency, ejection fraction and creatinine value at presentation, site of ST-elevation, number of leads with ST-elevation, and pre-hospital heart failure.
- *Therapeutic data*: Time of thrombolysis (door-to-needle time), time of angioplasty (door-to-balloon time), culprit lesion, ejection fraction, and therapy at discharge.

The eligible cohort consists then in all patients admitted to any hospitals of the Regione Lombardia Network with STEMI diagnosis.

4 The Lombardia Region Administrative Datawarehouse

In this section we describe structure, aim, and use of the Regione Lombardia Public Health Database (PHD), the datawarehouse the STEMI Archive has been designed to be integrated with. This is an ongoing datawarehouse, which up to now has been used only for administrative purposes, since decision makers of healthcare organizations need information about efficacy and costs of health services.

The PHD of Regione Lombardia contains a huge amount of data and requires specific and advanced tools for data mining and data analysis. The datawarehouse structure of PHD is called star scheme (see [10]), since it is centered on three main databases (*Ambulatoriale, Farmaceutica, Ricoveri*), containing information about visits, drugs, hospitalizations, and surgical procedures that took place during admission to hospitals, and it is supported by secondary databases (*Banca Dati Assistito* [*BDA*], *Medici, Codici Diagnosi e Procedure Chirurgiche*) which contain more specific and administrative information about drugs and procedures, coding personal information about people involved in the care process. The star scheme does not allow for repetitions in records entering: for example, just one record for each admission to hospital is allowed, and each record finishes with patient discharge. An *event* is the total of admissions and discharges related to the same episode of disease. Inside the PHD, several records may correspond to the same patient over time, even concerning the same event. A patient may have several events during years, and each event could consist of multiple admissions. For each admission/discharge path, one record is produced in PHD. Records related to the same subject may be linked in a temporal order to achieve the correct information about the basic observation unit (i.e., the individual patient/subject). However, each of databases described above has its own dimension and structure, and data are different and differently recorded from one database to another one. Suitable techniques are therefore required to make information coming from different databases uniform and not redundant. The longitudinal data that we will analyze will be generated by deterministic record linkage between STEMI Archive and the databases *Ambulatoriale, Farmaceutica, Ricoveri* and *BDA* of the PHD. Regione Lombardia data manager and owner provide an encrypted code for each patient in order to protect citizen's privacy. This encrypted code represents the key to obtain the deterministic linkage between the databases.

Once different sources of data have been linked, it is possible for clinicians, researchers, and people involved in healthcare governance to answer epidemiological questions such as the following: is the trigger event of the STEMI Archive the first cardiological event for the observed patient? If not, how many cardiovascular events have been recorded in the previous history of this patient? These information are provided by the integration of the STEMI Archive with *Ricoveri* administrative database. Moreover, if a patient is already known to the healthcare systems in terms of cardiovascular hospital admissions, was his/her therapy compliance good, i.e., did he/she assumed correct quantities of drugs and received a convenient treatment in terms of visits and clinical practice? These information are provided by the integration of the STEMI Archive with *BDA* and *Farmaci* administrative databases. Finally, how does the previous clinical history of each patient affect his/her outcome observed in the STEMI Archive gathering? These questions ask for a proper statistical modeling and represent the real and new challenges of the Strategic Program.

All the information coming from the integration let the researchers to point out new prognostic factors to be considered to better explain the main outcomes the hospitals are evaluated on. Then, the longer is the time slot on which the integration can be performed, the richer, the more complete, and the more reliable is the information which can be used in order to build the outcome measures. Regione Lombardia enabled us to look at the administrative datawarehouse up to 8 years ago. In such time slot, a single patient could have order of dozens admissions, hundreds of visits, drugs, and procedures. Dealing with such complex and high dimensional data is the challenge of the statistical analysis, as presented in Sect. 6.

5 Integration with Public Health Database

In this section we discuss the results of integration, in terms of the longitudinal electronic records obtained for each patient inserted in the STEMI Archive.

Over recent years, there has been an increasing agreement among epidemiologists on the validity of disease and intervention registries based on administrative databases (see [11–15]); this motivated Regione Lombardia to use its own administrative databases for clinical and epidemiological aims. In fact, even if randomized controlled trials (RCTs) remain the accepted "gold standard" for determining the efficacy of new drugs or medical procedures, they cannot provide alone all the relevant information that decision makers need in order to weigh the implications of particular policies affecting medical therapies. Research using disease and intervention registries, outcome studies using administrative databases, and performance indicators adopted by quality improvement methods can all shed light on who is most likely to benefit, what the important tradeoffs are, and how policy makers might promote the safe, effective, and appropriate use of new interventions.

Administrative healthcare databases can be analyzed in order to calculate measures of quality of care (quality indicators). The importance of this kind of database for clinical purposes depends on the fact that they provide all the relevant information that decision makers need to know, in order to evaluate the implications of particular policies affecting medical therapies (information about applicability of trial findings to the settings and patients of interest, effectiveness and widespread of new surgical techniques, estimation of adherence to best practice and potential benefits/harms of specific health policies, etc.). Moreover, administrative healthcare databases play today a central role in epidemiological evaluation of healthcare system because of their widespread diffusion and low cost of information.

When in the PHD we look for events related with a patient belonging to the population selected by the STEMI Archive (see Fig. 1), we find all his clinical history in terms of healthcare utilization (visits, hospital admissions, drugs, etc.). Since we are not interested in this huge amount of information, but only in cardiovascular events, criteria for choosing only the hospital discharge records effectively related to cardiovascular events are needed. In fact, the most critical issue when using administrative databases within observational studies is represented by the selection criteria of the discharge records: several different criteria may be used, and they will result in different images of prevalence or incidence of diseases. Among the most accepted criteria, those referring to the Agency for healthcare Research and Quality (AHRQ) methodology, the ones of

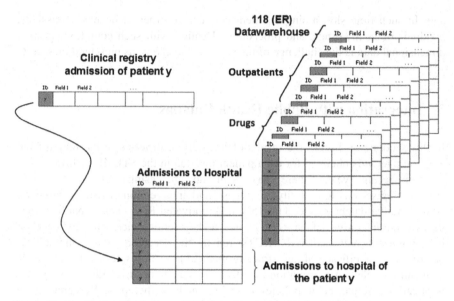

Fig. 1 Sketch of integration between STEMI Archive and public health database

Johns Hopkins Adjusted Clinical Groups (ACG), and Classification Research Groups (CRG) have been considered (for further details, see [16]).

As we said before, integrating clinical surveys on specific diseases with administrative databanks enables us to select subpopulation of interest for observational studies, focused on answering to specific epidemiological needs. In fact, the main point and the novelty of Strategic Program is the proposal of an epidemiological research for specific subpopulation of interest pointed out by clinical registries, which is different from the classical epidemiological inquiry since it is conducted starting from the Electronic Health Records, then it is faster and cheaper, and moreover it is real time achieving. For this new epidemiology, new methods for inquiry and analysis must be pointed out, and adequate information media must be provided. The STEMI Archive described in Sect. 3 and statistical models proposed in Sect. 6 are some of the instruments to be adopted to this aim, and the Strategic Program is the first official set in Italy where they have been considered. For further details on these topics, see [12, 13, 16–20].

As previously mentioned, when integration of different sources of data is performed, attention must be paid to a careful selection of covariates and data of interest. In this sense, further problems arise: firstly, as already mentioned, it is necessary to select only cardiovascular events and events in some way related to this pathology; then a dimensional reduction is needed, pointing out just covariates which can be of interest in exploiting outcomes by means of suitable covariates and process indicators. This is the challenge of the statistician, and it is strongly related with the clinical questions that physicians want to investigate. In this sense, several analyses can be performed on such rich and complex data. In the next section, we will give an overview of the potential of a statistical monitoring of data arising from integration of clinical registries and administrative databases.

6   The Role of Statistics

As mentioned before, such complex and huge databases ask for continuous monitoring and advanced statistical tools to be applied for evaluating outcomes and especially for pointing out the relationship between process indicators, patients' case mix, hospitals' exposure, and outcomes.

In fact, as can be evinced by the diagram reported in Fig. 2, a statistical analysis is helpful whenever it is necessary to:

- Inform policy making at regional level about the healthcare system efficiency and efficacy, in order to support their decisions with clear and well-defined evaluations procedures.
- Improve the quality of care, enhancing those patterns of care which have been proved to be the most effective in improving outcomes of patients.
- Identify poor performers.
- Provide hospital information to enable them to set strategies and policies in order to improve their service.
- Provide consumer information to facilitate choice of healthcare provider.

In order to do this, it is necessary to point out what causes variation in outcomes between healthcare providers, and this can be obtained from the analysis of data described in the previous sections.

6.1   Analysis of STEMI Archive Data

The preliminary data collection, carried out to test how the new integrated system would have worked, has been performed during the time slot from January to December 2010. It consists of 1,087 patients, admitted in 31 hospitals of Regione Lombardia with STEMI diagnosis. The population is stratified according to the expected results which can be found in the literature: in particular, the mean age and standard deviation are, respectively, 65.75 and 13.08 years (first, second, and third quantiles are respectively equal to 56, 66, and 75 years, i.e., more than a quarter of subjects is elder than 70), with men significantly younger than women (63.07 vs. 72.74 years, Wilcoxon nonparametric test p-value $<2.2 \times 10^{-16}$); concerning sex, males are 786, whereas females are 301, i.e., 72.3 % vs. 27.7 %. Moreover, 82 % of patients present the less severe infarction, indicated by Killip class I, 11 % have Killip class equal to II, 3.4 % equal to III, and 3.6 % are in the most severe class, the Killip class IV. Among these people, 41 % are smokers, 18 % are affected also by diabetes, and 61 % are high blood pressure sufferers. Furthermore, 81.5 %

Fig. 2 Flow chart of
statistical monitoring and
evaluation process in
healthcare systems

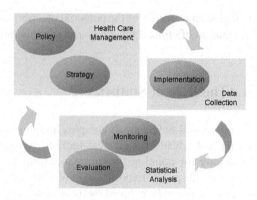

of the overall subjects underwent to primary PTCA. Only 4.5 % of people have
been treated with pharmacological therapy, as we expected since the cardiological
network of hospitals is oversized with respect to the territorial extension and then it
often happens that there is a hospital near enough to make the interventional
practice preferable to the pharmacological treatment. Finally, 1,039 patients
(95.6 %) are alive at discharge, and 78 % of the overall patients treated surgically
had positive outcome in terms of reperfusion (ST-segment resolution greater than
70 % after 1 hour from the intervention).

For all the patients inserted in the STEMI Archive during this test period,
integration with the administrative datawarehouse has been performed (for all
patients the deterministic link has been successful). The analyses have been focused
on different clinical issues. For example, from integration with the database
Farmaci, it is possible to check for the compliance to the prescribed therapy for
patients labeled as "known" to the cardiovascular events. A patient is defined
"known" if the oldest prescription for cardiovascular drugs contained in the administrative datawarehouse is elder than 1 year from the date of STEMI Archive
hospital admission. For these patients it is possible to check if they really bought
and then consumed enough quantity of drugs, and then if there is statistical evidence
to say that the poorer is the compliance, the higher is the readmission probability.
On the other hand, from integration of STEMI Archive with the database *Ricoveri*,
information about length and frequency of previous hospital admissions for each
patient can be pointed out, in order to perform survival analysis on time to the next
admission. In particular, 716 of the overall 1,087 patients of the STEMI Archive
(i.e., 75.86 %) are present in the database *Farmaci*, and 539 of them can be defined
"known" in the sense we explained above. On the other hand, 903 patients of the
STEMI Archive (83 %) have almost a previous hospital admission recorded in the
administrative datawarehouse, but only 546 of them have almost one previous
admission for cardiovascular diseases. This latter information can be obtained
from integration with *BDA* database, where information on category which the
admission belongs to can be found, together with codes labeling the category the
admission belongs to, as well as information on procedures and diagnoses.

It is therefore mandatory to perform sensitivity analysis to evaluate the validity of the estimates. Statistical analysis can be performed by means of multiple logistic regression models for studying outcomes and by means of survival analysis when studying failure times (hospital readmissions, continuity of drug prescriptions, survival times). Multilevel models can also be adopted if structural and organizational variables are measured. When outcomes are the main focus of the observational study, appropriate risk adjustment tools are needed. In particular effective variable selection is of paramount importance. Nonparametric partitioning methods, like CART (Classification and Regression Trees), tests on independence between predictors, and explorative data mining will highlight possible dependence patterns between covariates (e.g., see [2]).

Moreover, data coming from health databases are usually affected by a huge variability, called overdispersion. The main cause for this phenomenon is the grouped nature of data: each patient is a grouping factor with respect to his/her own admissions to hospital, while hospitals are a grouping factor with respect to admitted patients and so on. So one can model the primary and secondary outcomes using hospitals as grouping factor, so that a sort of implicit ranking/classification of providers can be provided directly by the adopted models. In fact, after splitting the effect on outcome due to the hospital from the outcome variability due to the different case mix, it is possible to generate health performance indicators and benchmarks that will make hospitals aware of their standing in the wider regional context. Such indexes of performances also enable healthcare governance to rank providers, to evaluate their performances, and to plan activities in order to invest in quality improvement. In this sense, integration between different sources of clinical information and complex databases is a good and useful instrument for health governance. In our case, overdispersion is detectable in the outcome variable. This can be due to several different causes. One of the most reasonable to consider is the difference in terms of number of patients yearly treated by the not negligible number of hospitals (31) involved in the study. It is known from clinical literature that health outcomes at different institutions could vary for random variation, for systematic influences of institutions or covariates on outcomes, or for the health of patient populations prior to admission. Generalized linear mixed models (GLMMs), i.e., generalized linear models with binary response (in-hospital survival) and generalized additive mixed models (GAMMs) with an additive random effect [21–23], are suitable statistical methods, both in a frequentist and Bayesian framework, to quantify the effect of the covariates on survival probability, taking the hospital of admission as a grouping factor and assuming it as parametric [24, 25] or nonparametric [26, 27] random effect.

Moreover, observing how the hospital behavior affects the survival probability, we would like to rank providers or to compare their performances with benchmarks gold standards. Procedures for analyzing and comparing healthcare provider effects on health services delivery and outcomes have been referred to as *provider profiling*. In a typical profiling procedure, patient-level responses are measured for clusters of patients treated by different providers. Then, firstly, the in-hospital survival rates are to be estimated by fitting parametric or semiparametric generalized linear mixed effects models (an example of such modeling performed adopting a Dirichlet process can be found in [28]). Then the comparison among providers' performances can be carried out through unsupervised classification algorithms, like k-means or similar [29]. Finally, decisional criteria for classification can be pointed out minimizing the expected loss arising from misclassification costs, for example, using Bayesian optimal decision rules (see [28]).

On the other hand, concerning integrated data, the main focus is the hospitalization's process of patients. In fact, it is possible to model these data as trajectories of a point process (see, e.g., [30]). The great challenge in doing this starting from integrated database and not only from the PHD datawarehouse is that an overcome of main problems concerning observational studies can be reached: in fact, using information of the previous patient history, we can account for case mix, while observational studies in general do not allow researchers to do this. Moreover, the linkage between information coming from registry and administrative data makes possible to insert estimates of clinical history of patients (resumed, e.g., by estimated hazard functions of readmission for each patient) in a wider semiparametric model constructed to explain and predict the main outcomes.

7 Conclusions and Open Problems

In this work we present and describe the STEMI Archive, as an example of multicenter observational clinical registry planned and designed to be integrated with administrative datawarehouse of Regione Lombardia. The link between the two databases will generate the primary platform for the study of impact and care of STEMI on the whole regional district we are concerned to. Previous data gathering and statistical analysis restricted to the urban area of Milano were compelling for the realization of this complex and challenging project.

We showed how the creation of an efficient regional network to face the ST-segment Elevation Myocardial Infarction is made possible by the design of the STEMI Archive and its integration with the regional Public Health Database: in fact this is the first platform for the study of impact and care of STEMI producing longitudinal data containing all the clinical history of patients of interest, which can be studied and resumed with statistical techniques we presented in Sect. 6. Moreover, provider profiling can be carried out on performance indicators, and they can be used to monitor and control healthcare offer of providers.

This innovative and pioneering experience stands as a candidate to become a methodological prototype for the optimization of healthcare processes in Regione Lombardia and to be extended in the future to different pathologies of interest, for their incidence and mortality, besides cardiovascular diseases.

Acknowledgments This work is within the Strategic Program "Exploitation, integration and study of current and future health databases in Lombardia for Acute Myocardial Infarction" supported by "Ministero del Lavoro, della Salute e delle Politiche Sociali" and by "Direzione

Generale Sanità—Regione Lombardia." The authors wish to thank the Working Group for Cardiac Emergency in Milano, the Cardiology Society, and the 118 Dispatch Center.

References

1. Grieco, N., Corrada, E., Sesana, G., Fontana, G., Lombardi, F., Ieva, F., Paganoni, A.M., Marzegalli, M.: Le reti dell'emergenza in cardiologia: l'esperienza lombarda. Giornale Italiano di Cardiologia, Supplemento "Crema Cardiologia 2008. Nuove Prospettive in Cardiologia," **9**, 56–62 (2008)
2. Ieva, F.: Modelli statistici per lo studio dei tempi di intervento nell'infarto miocardico acuto. Master thesis, Dipartimento di Matematica, Politecnico di Milano (2008). http://mox.polimi.it/it/progetti/pubblicazioni/tesi/ieva.pdf
3. Direzione Generale Sanità – Regione Lombardia. Determinazioni in merito alla "Rete per il trattamento dei pazienti con Infarto Miocardico con tratto ST elevato(STEMI)": Decreto N° 10446, 15/10/2009, Direzione Generale Sanità – Regione Lombardia
4. Fellegi, I., Sunter, A.: A theory for record linkage. J. Am. Stat. Assoc. **64**(328), 1183–1210 (1969)
5. Antman, E.M., Hand, M., Amstrong, P.W., Bates, E.R., Green, L.A., et al.: Update of the ACC/AHA 2004 guidelines for the management of patients with ST elevation myocardial infarction. Circulation **117**, 269–329 (2008)
6. Krumholz, H.M., Anderson, J.L., Bachelder, B.L., Fesmire, F.M.: ACC/AHA 2008 performance measures for adults with ST-elevation and non-ST-elevation myocardial infarction. Circulation **118**, 2596–2648 (2008)
7. Masoudi, F.A., Bonow, R.O., Brindis, R.G., Cannon, C.P., et al.: ACC/AHA 2008 statement on performance measurement and reperfusion therapy: a report of the ACC/AHA task force on performance measures (work group to address the challenges of performance measurement and reperfusion therapy). Circulation **118**, 2649–2661 (2008)
8. Ting, H.H., Krumholtz, H.M., Bradley, E.H., Cone, D.C., Curtis, J.P., et al.: Implementation and integration of prehospital ECGs into system of care for acute coronary syndrome. Circulation **118**, 1066–1079 (2008)
9. Oltrona, L., Mafrici, A., Marzegalli, M., Fiorentini, C., Pirola, R., Vincenti, A.: a nome dei Partecipanti allo Studio GestIMA e della Sezione Regionale Lombarda dell'ANMCO e della SIC: la gestione della fase iperacuta dell'infarto miocardico con sopraslivellamento del tratto ST nella Regione Lombardia (GestIMA). Ital. Heart J. Suppl. **6**, 489–497 (2005)
10. Inmon, W.H.: Building the data warehouse, 2nd edn. Wiley, New York, NY (1996)
11. Barendregt, J.J., Van Oortmarssen, J.G., Vos, T., et al.: A generic model for the assessment of disease epidemiology: the computational basis of DisMod II. Popul. Health Metr. **1**, 4 (2003)
12. Every, N.R., Frederick, P.D., Robinson, M., et al.: A comparison of the national registry of myocardial infarction with the cooperative cardiovascular project. J. Am. Coll. Cardiol. **33**(7), 1887–1894 (1999)
13. Hanratty, R., Estacio, R.O., Dickinson, L.M., et al.: Testing electronic algorithms to create disease registries in a safety net system. J. Health Care Poor Underserved **19**(2), 452–465 (2008)
14. Manuel, D.G., Lim, J.J.Y., Tanuseputro, P., et al.: How many people have a myocardial infarction? Prevalence estimated using historical hospital data. BMC Public Health **7**, 174–89 (2007)
15. Wirehn, A.B.., Karlsson, H.M., Cartensen, J.M., et al.: Estimating disease prevalence using a population-based administrative healthcare database. Scand. J. Public Health **35**, 424–431 (2007)

16. Barbieri, P., Grieco, N., Ieva, F., Paganoni, A.M., Secchi, P.: Exploitation, integration and statistical analysis of Public Health Database and STEMI archive in Lombardia Region. Complex data modeling and computationally intensive statistical methods – Series "Contribution to Statistics," Springer (2010)
17. Ieva, F., Paganoni, A.M.: Statistical analysis of an integrated database concerning patients with acute coronary syndromes. In: SCo2009, Sixth Conference – Proceedings, Maggioli editore, Milano (2009)
18. Glance, L.G., Osler, T.M., Mukamel, D.B., et al.: Impact of the present-on-admission indicator on hospital quality measurement experience with the agency for healthcare research and quality (AHRQ) inpatient quality indicators. Med. Care **46**(2), 112–119 (2008)
19. Hughes, J.S., Averill, R.F., Eisenhandler, J., et al.: Clinical risk groups (CRGs): a classification system for risk-adjusted capitation-based payment and health care management. Med. Care **42**(1), 81–90 (2004)
20. Sibley, L.M., Moineddin, R., Agham, M.M., et al.: Risk adjustment using administrative data-based and survey-derived methods for explaining physician utilization. Med. Care **48**, 175–182 (2010)
21. Goldstein, H.: Multilevel statistical models. Arnolds, London (2003)
22. Mc Cullagh, P., Nelder, J.A.: Generalized linear models. Chapman & Hall/CRC, New York, NY (2000)
23. Hastie, T.J., Tibshirani, R.J.: Generalized additive models. Chapman & Hall/CRC, New York, NY (1999)
24. Ieva, F., Paganoni, A.M.: Multilevel models for clinical registers concerning STEMI patients in a complex urban reality: a statistical analysis of MOMI^2 survey. Commun. Appl. Ind. Math. **1**(1), 128–147 (2010)
25. Guglielmi, A., Ieva, F., Paganoni, A.M., Ruggeri, F.: A Bayesian random-effects model for survival probabilities after acute myocardial infarction. Chil. J. Stat. **3**(1), 1–15 (2012)
26. Aitkin, M.: A general maximum likelihood analysis of variance components in generalized linear models. Biometrics **55**, 117–128 (1999)
27. Grieco, N., Ieva, F., Paganoni, A.M.: Performance assessment using mixed effects models: A case study on coronary patient care. IMA. J. Manag. Math. **23**(2), 117–131 (2012)
28. Guglielmi, A., Ieva, F., Paganoni, A.M., Ruggeri, F.: Process indicators and outcome measures in the treatment of acute myocardial infarction patients. In: Faltin, R., Kenett, F., Ruggeri, F. (eds) Statistical Methods in Healthcare, chap. 10, pp. 219–229. Wiley, Chichester (2012)
29. Hartigan, J.A., Wong, M.A.: A K-means clustering algorithm. Appl. Stat. **28**, 100–108 (1979)
30. Baraldo, S., Ieva, F., Paganoni, A.M., Vitelli, V.: Generalized functional linear models for recurrent events: an application to re-admission processes in heart failure patients. Scand. J. Stat. (2013). doi:10.1111/j.1467-9469.2012.00818.x

Statistical Methods to Study the Representativeness of STEMI Archive

Giovanni Cassarini and Francesca Ieva

Abstract Direzione Generale Sanità, Regione Lombardia, funded in January 2009 the Strategic Program "Exploitation, integration and study of current and future health databases in Lombardia for Acute Myocardial Infarction." The aim of this project was the integration and the statistical analysis of complex clinical and administrative databases. In this context the STEMI Archive was created in collaboration with Politecnico di Milano and several hospital structures. This archive contains clinical data about patients affected by acute myocardial infarction with ST elevation (STEMI) admitted in any hospital of Regione Lombardia. In this chapter we will discuss the representativeness of the sample of patients registered in the archive compared with the overall population of STEMI patients affected by acute myocardial infarction, extracted from the administrative database of the Regione Lombardia.

1 Introduction

A particular and very serious type of acute myocardial infarction is characterized by an abnormal elevation of the ST segment on the electrocardiogram. The disease called ST elevation myocardial infarction (STEMI) is caused by an occlusion of the coronary artery that causes an ischemia and a lack of supply of oxygen to the cardiac cells. These effects, if not promptly treated, may cause a damage of the cardiac tissue (myocardium), up to cause a heart attack. In order to analyze and

G. Cassarini (✉)
MoxOff, Spin Off del Politecnico di Milano, P.za Leonardo da Vinci 32, Milan 20133, Italy
e-mail: giovanni.cassarini@moxoff.com

F. Ieva
Dipartimento di Matematica, MOX, Politecnico di Milano, P.za Leonardo da Vinci 32, Milan 20133, Italy
e-mail: francesca.ieva@mail.polimi.it

N. Grieco et al. (eds.), *New Diagnostic, Therapeutic and Organizational Strategies for Acute Coronary Syndromes Patients*, Contributions to Statistics,
DOI 10.1007/978-88-470-5379-3_4, © Springer-Verlag Italia 2013

optimize the current treatment programs for the care and prevention of STEMI, the "Direzione Generale Sanità, Regione Lombardia," with Politecnico di Milano and several hospitals, has funded and supported the construction of the STEMI Archive (see [1] and [2]), a clinical registry aimed at collecting specialized information to describe in detail the STEMI event. Moreover, Regione Lombardia stores in its administrative Public Health Database (PHD) all the information about diagnoses and surgical procedures of all the patients admitted to any hospital. These informations, gathered for the administrative purpose of refunding hospitals for these services and not for clinical and epidemiological tracking, are collected in a database held by the Direzione Generale Sanità, which will be called "administrative database." To each hospitalization is associated a record (called *Scheda di Dimissione Ospedaliera, SDO*). In these records each disease or intervention is coded so that it is interpreted according to international standards (see [3]).

2   Definition and Construction of the STEMI Archive

This section will describe the objectives and contents of the STEMI Archive, the clinical registry on STEMI that collects data concerning all the hospital admission of patients affected by ST segment elevation myocardial infarction. Each record can be divided into four categories, each concerning:

1. *Personal information*: Encrypted version of identity code, date of birth, sex, weight, height, and hospital where admitted.
2. *Preadmission data*: Risk factors (like diabetes, smoke, hypertension, high cholesterol, previous heart diseases).
3. *Admission data*: Time and type of symptoms, time of first call to the doctor, time to call for rescue, type of rescue unit sent, time of first ECG, site of infarction on ECG, admission parameters, fast-track activation, Killip class (to quantify the severity of the infarction), blood pressure, heart rate, ejection fraction and creatinine value at presentation, site of ST elevation, number of leads with ST elevation, and prehospital heart failure.
4. *Therapeutic data and outcomes*: Time of thrombolysis (door-to-needle time), time of angioplasty (door-to-balloon time), culprit lesion, MACE, ejection fraction and therapy at discharge, ST resolution, and in-hospital mortality.

As mentioned earlier, the design of STEMI Archive comes from collaboration between the Direzione Generale Sanità, Regione Lombardia, Politecnico di Milano, and several hospitals. The structures that joined the project are listed in Table 1, together with the number of cases inserted in the collection.

The STEMI Archive was built using data collected in three phases: the first one from January to December 2010, the second one from January to June 2011, and the third one from October to December 2011.

Table 1 Structures having a role in building the STEMI Archive

Code	Structure name	Location	Cases
030194	Ospedale Civile	Voghera	24
030193	Ospedale Civile	Vigevano	22
030006	Ospedale S. Antonio Abate	Gallarate	42
030908	Istituti Ospitalieri	Cremona	80
030913	Ospedale Niguarda Ca' Granda	Milano	89
030004	Ospedale di Circolo	Busto Arsizio	12
030008	Ospedale Provinciale Generale	Saronno	23
030010	Ospedale di Circolo Galmarini	Tradate	46
030209	Ospedale Maggiore	Crema	36
030901	Ospedale di Circolo e Fondazione Macchi	Varese	59
030085	Causa Pia Ospitaliera Uboldo	Cernusco SN	17
030072	Ospedale di Circolo Predabissi	Vizzolo Predabissi	12
030910	Ospedale Fatebenefratelli e Oftalmico	Milano	15
030281	Ospedale di Legnano	Legnano	121
030074	Ospedale G. Fornaroli	Magenta	33
030154	Presidio Ospedaliero di Chiari	Chiari	66
030916	Ospedale L. Sacco	Milano	46
030073	Ospedale di Circolo	Rho	90
030066	Ospedale G. Salvini	Garbagnate	1
030915	Ospedale S. Carlo Borromeo	Milano	77
030909	Ospedale S. Gerardo	Monza	106
030914	Ospedale S. Paolo	Milano	80
030140	Ospedale Bolognini	Seriate	7
030906	Presidio Ospedaliero Spedali Civili	Brescia	70
030068	Ospedale di Circolo	Desio	4
030157	Ospedale Civile "La Memoria di Gavardo"	Gavardo	15
030184	Ospedale di Manerbio	Manerbio	29
030907	Presidio Ospedaliero "C. Poma"	Mantova	77
030274	Ospedale Valcamonica	Esine	51
030042	Ospedale Civile	Sondrio	48
030079	Ospedale Civico	Codogno	13
030067	Ospedale Maggiore	Lodi	4
030935	S. Raffaele	Milano	4
030295	Poliambulanza	Brescia	14
030058	Ospedale Bassini	Cinisello Balsamo	58
030936	Istituto Auxologico Italiano—I.S. S.Luca	Milano	54
030147	Policlinico S. Marco	Osio Sotto	8
030943	Istituto Clinico Humanitas	Rozzano	68
030924	Ospedale Policlinico S. Matteo	Pavia	51
030903	Ospedale di Circolo "A. Manzoni"	Lecco	144
030925	Fondazione IRCCS OM Policlinico	Milano	46
030905	Ospedali Riuniti	Bergamo	17
030112	Istituto Clinico S. Ambrogio	Milano	3
	Total		1,882

3   The Administrative Database

The administrative database encompasses the real whole population of acute myocardial infarction in Regione Lombardia. This database contains all the information concerning each hospital admission for any disease and related practices. Each record of administrative database contains, among all the other information, six fields devoted to register the diagnoses of the patient in that admission. These diagnoses are coded according to the international standards of ICD9-CM, so it is possible to reconstruct complex pathologies the patient is affected by assembling these codes in a suitable way. There are different criteria for reconstructing the diseases (and AMI among these) from the diagnosis and intervention codes recorded within the SDO. Starting from hospital discharge records in the administrative database, two are the most frequently used and reliable criteria adopted for the epidemiological goal of pointing of the population of AMI patients: ASSR and CCM. According to these, the encoding of AMI can be carried as follows:

- *ASSR:* Consider as related to an AMI patient any record containing one of the codes reported in Table 2 as primary diagnosis
- *CCM:* Analog to the ASSR criterion, but considering the codes in Table 2 to be present in any of the six diagnosis fields, under the condition that the primary diagnosis is one of those reported in Table 3

We may notice that CCM criterion labels as AMI patients more cases than ASSR does, because heart attacks deriving from complications of other pathologies are considered, too. In particular, the comparison with the STEMI Archive has been made, considering four different populations extracted from the administrative database:

ASSR06	ASSR with the third digit of diagnosis code $\in \{0,\ldots,6\}$
ASSR0689	ASSR with the third digit of diagnosis code $\in \{0,\ldots,6, 8, 9\}$
CCM06	CCM with the third digit of diagnosis code $\in \{0,\ldots,6\}$
CCM0689	CCM with the third digit of diagnosis code $\in \{0,\ldots,6, 8, 9\}$

4   Representativeness of the STEMI Archive

The objective of this work is to assess the representativeness of STEMI Archive subpopulation compared with administrative database whole population. In order to make a significance comparison, we need to select common variables between the two databases. According to clinical suggestions, we selected:

- Patient age and gender
- Patient status at discharge

Table 2 ICD9-CM codes identifying AMI

Code	Diagnosis
41000	AMI of anterolateral wall—episode of care unspecified
41001	AMI of anterolateral wall—initial episode of care
41010	AMI of other anterior wall—episode of care unspecified
41011	AMI of other anterior wall—initial episode of care
41020	AMI of inferolateral wall—episode of care unspecified
41021	AMI of inferolateral wall—initial episode of care
41030	AMI of inferoposterior wall—episode of care unspecified
41031	AMI of inferoposterior wall—initial episode of care
41040	AMI of inferior wall—episode of care unspecified
41041	AMI of inferior wall—initial episode of care
41050	AMI of other lateral wall—episode of care unspecified
41051	AMI of other lateral wall—initial episode of care
41060	AMI true posterior wall infarction—episode of care unspecified
41061	AMI true posterior wall infarction—initial episode of care
41080	AMI of other specified sites—episode of care unspecified
41081	AMI of other specified sites—initial episode of care
41090	AMI unspecified sites—episode of care unspecified
41091	AMI unspecified sites—initial episode of care

Table 3 ICD9-CM codes for CCM criterion

Code	Diagnosis
4271	Paroxysmal ventricular tachycardia
42741	Ventricular fibrillations
42742	Ventricular flutter
4275	Cardiac arrest
4281	Left heart failure
4295	Rupture of chordae tendineae
4296	Rupture of papillary muscle
42971	Acquired cardiac septal defect
42979	Other certain sequelae of myocardial infarction, not elsewhere classified
42981	Other disorders of papillary muscle
5184	Acute edema of lung, unspecified
7802	Syncope and collapse
78551	Cardiogenic shock
41410	Aneurysm of heart (wall)
4230	Hemopericardium

To verify the representativeness of the STEMI Archive compared to the real population, statistical tests for comparing proportions have been carried out:

- Comparison of proportions considering the totality of population affected by AMI for the variables:

  - *Gender*—man, woman
  - *Status at discharge*—alive, deceased

- Comparison of proportions considering separately male and female population affected by AMI for the variable:
  - *Status at discharge*—alive, deceased
- Comparison of means for the variable **age** considering the following categories:
  - Totality of population
  - Men
  - Women
  - Alive
  - Deceased
  - Alive men
  - Deceased men
  - Alive women
  - Deceased women

4.1 Results and Conclusions

In this section the results of the analysis explained above are reported, without taking into account the split for specific hospital structure. Tables 4 and 5 are represented with the value of each variable we mentioned before within the subpopulation represented in the STEMI Archive and the value of the same variable within the whole population of administrative database. The STEMI cases in the administrative database have been extracted according to ASSR0689, ASSR06, CCM0689, and CCM06 criteria.

Looking at the results of Tables 4 and 5, we recall that the quality of data has been impacted by the knowledge of procedures, discipline, and habits in filling the forms by the hospital operators.

We can observe that the sample fits in a better way with ASSR06 family. This means that the archive representativeness of the population of patient subjected to acute myocardial infarction is higher when a more restrictive filtering criterion is selected. This can be explained observing that ICD9CM codes with final digit equal to eight or nine have not been inserted in the archive. Since these codes represent patients where characteristics of heart attack are not well specified because they are affected by multiple pathologies in addition to AMI, their presence is likely to influence strongly the features of the sample. We suppose that hospital operators record in the archive only the patients data where the disease is clearly identified as first diagnosis. For this reason we can say that the STEMI Archive contains a subset of the total population, and we suggest for the next future to push so that the hospital organizations will fill completely the archive with all the patients records.

Table 4 Comparison between STEMI Archive and ASSR0689 and ASSR06 populations

Variable	STEMI Archive	ASSR0689	ASSR06
% Men	71.79 %	63.71 %	66.53 %
% Women	28.21 %	36.29 %	33.47 %
% Alive	94.79 %	91.79 %	91.05 %
% Deceased	5.21 %	8.21 %	8.95 %
% Alive (M)	95.93 %	93.71 %	93.55 %
% Deceased (M)	4.07 %	6.29 %	6.45 %
% Alive (W)	91.90 %	88.42 %	86.07 %
% Deceased (W)	8.10 %	11.58 %	13.93 %
Mean age	66.083	70.010	67.945
Mean age (M)	63.264	66.295	64.188
Mean age (W)	73.23	76.532	75.414
Mean age (A)	65.575	69.134	66.869
Mean age (D)	75.333	79.798	78.888
Mean age (M,A)	63.023	65.613	63.432
Mean age (M,D)	69.188	76.454	75.143
Mean age (W,A)	72.352	75.686	74.294
Mean age (W,D)	83.194	82.986	82.336

M = men, W = women, A = alive, D = deceased

Table 5 Comparison between STEMI Archive and CCM0689 and CCM06 populations

Variable	STEMI Archive	CCM0689	CCM06
% Men	71.79 %	63.49 %	66.30 %
% Women	28.21 %	36.51 %	33.70 %
% Alive	94.79 %	91.07 %	90.29 %
% Deceased	5.21 %	8.93 %	9.71 %
% Alive (M)	95.93 %	93.08 %	92.92 %
% Deceased (M)	4.07 %	6.92 %	7.08 %
% Alive (W)	91.90 %	87.57 %	85.12 %
% Deceased (W)	8.10 %	12.43 %	14.88 %
Mean age	66.083	70.160	68.081
Mean age (M)	63.264	66.426	64.297
Mean age (W)	73.23	76.652	75.527
Mean age (A)	65.575	69.231	66.936
Mean age (D)	75.333	79.634	78.726
Mean age (M,A)	63.023	65.695	63.484
Mean age (M,D)	69.188	76.265	74.957
Mean age (W,A)	72.352	75.766	74.351
Mean age (W,D)	83.194	82.892	82.256

M = men, W = women, A = alive, D = deceased

4.2   Further Developments

In order to go further in the analysis, we are considering a comparison among the comorbidity score (index of severity of pathologies before the myocardial infarction) arising from STEMI Archive and the one arising from administrative database. This comparison is complex to be performed since we need to make the comorbidity score computed on data in the administrative database comparable with the one computed on data in the STEMI Archive. To this purpose, we need to identify a transformation factor that allows us to make the two score measurements comparable. As a starting point we can assume that this transformation factor could depend from the weight of each pathology on the welfare of the patient.

In conclusion, in this work we showed how an administrative database may be used for addressing epidemiological issues as well as validating clinical survey. We believe that this paradigm should be considered by people in charge with healthcare governance, since it is sustainable, flexible, and effective, enabling planning and resources allocation to be based on real evidence and needs.

References

1. Ieva, F.: Designing and mining a multicenter observational clinical registry concerning patients with acute coronary syndromes. http://www1.mate.polimi.it/biblioteca/qddview.php?id= 1443&L=i (2012, submitted online)
2. Decreto No 20592, 11/02/2005, Direzione Generale Sanità – Regione Lombardia (2005), Patologie cardiocerebrovascolari: interventi di prevenzione, diagnosi e cura
3. http://www.ahrq.gov, site of Agency for Healthcare Research and Quality, U.S. Department of Health and Human Services
4. Barbieri, P., Grieco, N., Ieva, F., Paganoni, A.M., Secchi, P.: Exploitation, integration and statistical analysis of public health database and STEMI archive in Lombardia Region. Complex data modeling and computationally intensive statistical methods – "Series Contribution to Statistics", pp. 41–56. Springer (2010)
5. Decreto No 10446, 15/10/2009, Direzione Generale Sanità – Regione Lombardia (2009), Determinazioni in merito alla Rete per il trattamento dei pazienti con Infarto Miocardico con tratto ST elevato (STEMI)

Using Text Mining to Validate Diagnoses of Acute Myocardial Infarction

Stefano Ballerio and Dario Cerizza

Abstract We applied text mining to a database of discharge letters of patients with acute myocardial infarction for a quality of care-related task: the automatic validation of acute myocardial infarction diagnoses. The system should evaluate if the information contained in the discharge letters was consistent, by medical standards, with the letters' coded diagnoses of acute myocardial infarction. The system was composed of a text mining tool (GATE) and a set of linguistic resources which were specifically developed from a training set of letters. It was validated on a test set of letters manually annotated by cardiologists and results were satisfactory. Further analyses can be made on the efficiency of the development of the system and on its ongoing effectiveness.

1 Context, Objectives, and Methodology

"Text Mining can be broadly defined as a knowledge-intensive process in which a user interacts with a document collection over time by using a suite of analysis tools. In a manner analogous to data mining, text mining seeks to extract useful information from data sources through the identification and exploration of interesting patterns. In the case of text mining, however, the data sources are document collections, and interesting patterns are found not among formalized database records but in the unstructured textual data in the documents in these collections" [1]. In recent years, text mining (TM) has been applied to electronic patient records and other clinical documents for a variety of tasks, such as investigating adverse

---

S. Ballerio (✉)
Azienda Ospedaliera di Melegnano, Melegnano (MI), Italy
e-mail: stefano.ballerio@gmail.com

D. Cerizza
CEFRIEL, ICT Institute Politecnico di Milano, Milan, Italy
e-mail: dario.cerizza@cefriel.com

N. Grieco et al. (eds.), *New Diagnostic, Therapeutic and Organizational Strategies for Acute Coronary Syndromes Patients*, Contributions to Statistics,
DOI 10.1007/978-88-470-5379-3_5, © Springer-Verlag Italia 2013

drug reactions [2], monitoring and preventing adverse events [3], automatically identifying radiology reports containing critical results [4], extracting information to diagnose post-traumatic stress disorder [5], and much more. The project we present falls within this stream of researches. It was part of a larger project called *Exploitation, integration and study of current and future health databases on acute coronary syndromes in Lombardy*.[1] The overall aim of the project was integrating and exploiting health system databases and building thematical records for acute coronary syndromes. In this context, we conjectured that TM might be applied to databases on Acute Myocardial Infarction (AMI) for a quality of care-related task: the automatic validation of AMI diagnoses. Though administrative databases usually contain little information on diagnoses, in fact, textual databases, and discharge letters (DLs) in particular, can contain much information of this kind. Thus, we planned to develop a TM system that could process the DLs of patients with a coded diagnosis of AMI and evaluate if the information they contained, by medical standards, was consistent with the coded diagnoses of AMI the DLs were related to. All patients who receive a diagnosis of AMI, in fact, are given an ICD-9-CM diagnostic code specific for AMI. By medical standards, moreover, a diagnosis of AMI should be supported by the recognition of specific diagnostic elements, which should be mentioned in the patient's DL. Thus, the system would check if the DLs of patients with a coded diagnosis of AMI actually contained these diagnostic elements or not (as we will explain later, we also applied the system to DLs that were related to diagnoses different from AMI, to check if they contained diagnostic elements which might have supported a diagnosis of AMI).

In Sect. 2, we will introduce the medical standards that guided our research as to the diagnostic elements and hence the information to search for in the DLs. In Sect. 3, we will explain how we developed the system: first, we composed a training set of DLs to develop the system and a test set of DLs to apply the system to once it had been developed; second, we selected a TM tool (our system would be composed by this tool and by the linguistic resources we would develop); third, the DLs of the training set were manually annotated by cardiologists, who annotated all the portions of text that contained information useful to develop and refine the linguistic resources the system would use to automatically annotate the DLs; fourth, we developed the linguistic resources (lexicons and grammars) the system would use to process the DLs; fifth, we applied the system to the DLs of the test set, compared its answers with a gold standard provided by cardiologists, and measured its performance. In Sect. 4, we will discuss and evaluate the results of the system. In Sect. 5, finally, we will briefly consider some possible developments of the system.

---

[1] The project was financed by Regione Lombardia. The TM section was realized by Azienda Ospedaliera di Melegnano, Politecnico di Milano, and CEFRIEL (CEFRIEL is a not-for-profit organization. Its shareholders are universities, public authorities, and 15 leading multinational companies in ICT and media sectors. CEFRIEL's primary objective is to strengthen existing ties between academic and business worlds in the innovative ICT sector, by carrying out research and development in application fields that today are crucial for enterprises and public authorities).

2 Medical Standards and System Requirements

Our TM system should search for diagnostic information. By World Health Organization standards, when a diagnosis of AMI is formulated, at least two of these three types of diagnostic elements should be present:

1. Electrocardiographic evidence (some ECG results can be associated with AMI, while others cannot or aren't specific enough).
2. Myocardial markers from blood tests (blood tests must show that certain enzymes, such as troponin, have certain values).
3. Specific forms of chest pain (e.g., a pain that goes from the left shoulder to the throat can be a symptom of infarction; a pain in the lower-right part of the back is not).

Moreover, secondary elements such as algid perspiration might also be present.

Our TM system would therefore process the DLs searching for mentions of these primary and secondary diagnostic elements. Then, for each DL it would record the number of primary and secondary elements, checking whether at least two primary elements were mentioned and which ones.

Diagnoses validation is used to improve the quality of care. It is usually performed by expert personnel (doctors or nurses) who examine the clinical documents of a sample of patients and search for any information useful to check the diagnoses formulated for the patients, just as our TM system should do. These personnel can grant excellent results, but the task is time-consuming and therefore expensive. An automated system might be more efficient and less expensive, but of course it can only be used if its accuracy and reliability have been ascertained. In general, a satisfactory trade-off between effectiveness and efficiency must be reached and this implied three system requirements:

1. The effectiveness of the system must be accurately evaluated in terms of precision and recall (the system must be accurate and reliable).
2. The processing of the DLs must be efficient in terms of time.
3. The development of the system must not be too time- and resource-consuming in relation to its subsequent use.

After describing the development and the application of the system, we will discuss its results and assess to what extent the requirements were met.

3 System Development, Application, and Evaluation

The process of development, application, and evaluation of the system was organized into five phases, as reported in Fig. 1.

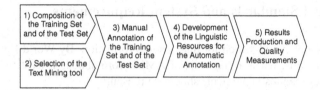

Fig. 1 The five-phase process adopted to develop and evaluate the system

3.1 Composition of the Training Set and of the Test Set

To develop the system and measure its performance, we extracted two sets of DLs from the databases of two hospitals[2]: the training set and the test set. The training set was used to develop, test, and refine the language resources (lexicons and grammars) the system would use to process the DLs. It was composed of DLs related to diagnoses of AMI that had been produced by the cardiology departments of the two hospitals. The test set was used to measure the performance of the system and to assess the quality of its results. It was composed of three subsets of DLs: AMI DLs from the cardiology departments, non-AMI DLs from the cardiology departments, and non-AMI DLs from other departments.

Table 1 shows the composition of the various sets, indicating for each set the number of DLs it was composed of, the years of production of the DLs, the diagnoses the DLs were related to, and the department they came from.

3.2 Selection of the Text Mining Tool

In parallel with the composition of the training set and of the test set, we performed a scouting to select the best suitable text mining tool to setup the system.

Four main requirements guided our scouting:

- Free software: we searched for free software, because a licensing cost would prevent other structures of the National Healthcare System from adopting our system.
- Provide functionalities for *lexical analysis*: the tool must be able to parse the DLs and tokenize words, tag them accordingly to their part of speech, and perform basic morphological analysis. As DLs are written in a specialized language, the tool must also accept configurable lexicons.
- Provide functionalities for *syntactic analysis*: the tool must be able to compare the syntactic structure of the text of the DLs with configurable grammars.

---

[2] Uboldo Hospital and Vizzoli Predabissi Hospital. Both of them are situated in Lombardy (Italy) and are part of Azienda Ospedaliera di Melegnano. To respect patients' privacy, all DLs were anonymized at the time of extraction.

Table 1 Composition of the training set and of the test set

Set	Number of DLs	Years of production	Diagnosis and department
Training set	288	2004–2010	AMI, from cardiology
Test set, subset 1	150	2004–2010	AMI, from cardiology
Test set, subset 2	75	2004–2010	Non-AMI, from cardiology
Test set, subset 3	75	2004–2010	Non-AMI, not from cardiology

- Easy to use graphical user interface: this would support users in performing the manual annotation of the DLs.

On the basis of these requirements, we identified in GATE [6] (General Architecture for Text Engineering) the most suitable tool.[3] GATE is an extensible architecture, shipped with several plug-ins that permit the examination of alternative solutions. GATE is also a well-adopted solution, running since 1995 and supported by a mature and extensive community of developers, users, and educators that can provide on-demand support.

3.3 Manual Annotation of the Training Set and of the Test Set

Two cardiologists manually annotated all the DLs using the GATE user interface. In each DL, they highlighted and annotated all the portions of text where primary or secondary diagnostic elements were mentioned.

The manual annotations attached by the cardiologists to the DLs of the training set were then used to develop and refine the linguistic resources the system would use to automatically annotate the DLs (see phase 4).

The manual annotations attached by the cardiologists to the DLs of the test set produced the gold standard for the evaluation of the system (see phase 5). The performance of the system would be measured by comparing the manually generated annotations attached to each DL with the automatically generated annotations attached to that same letter.

To correctly evaluate the performance of the system, the two sets of letters were kept separate: on one side, linguistic resources were developed using only the DLs of the training set; on the other side, the performance measures we will report and discuss are related to the application of the system to the DLs of the test set only.

---

[3] GATE is a project of the University of Sheffield and it is freely available as an open source software architecture at http://gate.ac.uk.

3.4   Development of the Linguistic Resources for the Automatic Annotation

The main goal of the system was the identification of all the occurrences of each diagnostic element within each DL. Ideally, the system must be able to detect all the occurrences of each diagnostic element (thus achieving a high *recall score*) and to not erroneously recognize occurrences of any diagnostic element in those parts of the DLs where there was none (thus achieving a high *precision score*).

The identification of the diagnostic elements implied the distinction among a wide variety of linguistic expressions that were used in the DLs and their classification into one of the categories of diagnostic elements. For example, the *chest pain* category could be instantiated in the DLs by different expressions, such as *pain in the sub-mammary area*, or *episode of angina*, or *pain radiating from the chest to the left shoulder and the throat*.[4] The system must be able to detect all three expressions and categorize them as *chest pain*. This meant reducing the linguistic variety of the DLs to few categories of interest.

From a linguistic point of view, the diversity of the DLs is due to two factors: lexical diversity and syntactic diversity (the same concept can be expressed with different words, or formulated into different syntactic structures, or both). To tackle this diversity, the system should use suitable lexicons and grammars. Such knowledge resources are often critical for TM systems and in the TM community there is a general awareness that appropriate resources are usually lacking [7]. This is particularly true if you are working with the Italian language and in fact we had to develop our own specific lexicons and grammars. Lexicons would provide information about the relevance of different words for different categories: words like *angina, pain, radiated,* and *chest*, for example, would be relevant for the *chest pain* category and *troponin* for the *blood markers* category. Grammars, contextualized to the categories of diagnostic elements, would formally define classes of expressions that should be treated as if they were the same though their syntactic structures were different: *chest pain* and *pain in the chest*, for example, should be treated as equivalent. Besides, they would state that certain words would be relevant for certain categories only if they were related to certain other words: for example, the word *pain* would be relevant for the *chest pain* category only if it were followed by expressions such as *chest* or *sub-mammary area* (and not, e.g.,, if it were followed by *in the leg*).

A preliminary analysis of the training set also showed that the system would have to face three challenges, due to the fact that the DLs were unstructured narratives, possibly dealing with the entire clinical history of the patients and produced in a clinical context where they would not undergo any linguistic or editorial standardization.

---

[4] The DLs were written in Italian, but we will translate quotations from them into English for better clarity.

The first challenge was the presence of negations that must be correctly recognized to avoid false positives. For example, the system must be able to determine that *the patient doesn't report chest pain* is not equivalent to *the patient reports chest pain*.

The second challenge was related to the necessity of distinguishing between information on the patient's past history and information on her or his recent history. Mentions of diagnostic elements are indeed contained in those parts of the DLs that summarize the patient's medical history and they must be distinguished from those related to the present admission, to which the coded diagnosis of the DL is related. For example, in *May 2001: patient admitted to Vizzolo hospital with evidence of myocardial infarction in the anterolateral area*, the system must not identify an occurrence of the *electrocardiographic evidence* diagnostic element, because the mention is related to the past history rather than the present admission.

The third challenge was related to the nonstandardization of the words actually used in the DLs, which contained many irregular expressions (*Things all right* or *Blood markers not ok, see attached docs*), abbreviations (*tp* or *tropo* for *troponin*, *AL* for *anterolateral*), and typos (*ST semgent evlelation* for *ST segment elevation*).

To face the first challenge, we composed a lexicon of negations and we configured the grammars so that they would define the scope of negations and thus recognize negated words. This means we included words and expressions like *not* or *in absence of* in the lexicon of negations and then configured the grammars so that they would annotate as *negated* all mentions of diagnostic elements that occurred within a certain distance from those negations. Distances were set in relation to what we could observe in the DLs of the training set, to the syntax of Italian, and to the different types of negations. We also took into account punctuation and words and expressions that might limit the scope of a negation, such as *except for* in *no chest pain except for a slight numbness of the left shoulder*.

For the second challenge, we developed lexicons and grammars that would recognize temporal expressions and markers such as weekdays' names, month names, sequences of numbers that can identify dates or past years, expressions that identify specific parts of the day, words that refer to chronic diseases, and more. This would help the system distinguish the information related to the patient's past history from that related to her or his recent history.

For the third challenge, we included in lexicons and grammars the irregular forms and typos we found most frequently in the DLs of the training set.

As we said, lexicons and grammars were manually developed using the annotated DLs of the training set.

A lexicon is a list of entries and each entry is a word form with semantic and morphological metadata. The following code is an excerpt from a lexicon that was used for the *chest pain* category:

```
pain & gnr = m & lemma = pain & nmb = s & pos = N
pains & gnr = m & lemma = pain & nmb = p & pos = N
oppression & gnr = f & lemma = oppression & nmb = s &
pos = N
```

In this example we have three entries, involving three forms (`pain`, `pains`, and `oppression`) for which the following metadata are specified: the gender (`gnr`), which can be masculine (`m`) or feminine (`f`); the term (`lemma`) to which the form is traced (`pain`, `oppression`); the number (`nmb`), which can be singular (`s`) or plural (`p`); and the part of speech (`pos`), which is noun (`n`) for all three forms. As they are included in a particular lexicon (for the *chest pain* category, as we said), all three forms are also tagged with semantic metadata which say that those forms are related to the `pain` semantic domain and to the `non specific pain` semantic domain in particular. The lexicon is coded in conformity with the rules of GATE.

For our project, we developed the following lexicons:

- Biomedical lexicons, with terms related to pain and other symptoms, body parts, electrocardiographic reports, and enzymes (1035 forms). Each biomedical lexicon had its own semantic tags.
- Lexicons of negations (with different tags for different types of negations), used by grammars to parse negations (739 forms).
- Lexicons of time-related terms (with different semantic tags), used by grammars to distinguish between the patient's past and present histories (89 forms).
- A lexicon of articles, prepositions, and conjunctions, which would be useful for some grammars (273 forms).

On the whole, our lexicons included 2,136 forms.

A grammar is a decision rule composed of two parts (a) a description, written in a formal language, of a class of linguistic expressions and (b) a set of metadata or annotations to be attached to those portions of text to which the description of the first part of the rule applies. Each rule, therefore, has this logical structure: if expression X belongs to the class of expressions I describe, then attach this annotation to X. The descriptions use the metadata of the lexical entries. In a natural language paraphrase, a simple rule might be something like this: if you find a sequence made up of a word with a `non specific pain` semantic tag and then, within five words, zero to one word with the `prep` (i.e., *preposition*) tag and one to three words with a `front upper body` semantic tag and no full stop in between, then attach the `pain in the chest` annotation to that sequence of words. Each rule is deterministic.

On the whole, 35 rules were defined.

Once we had lexicons and grammars, we developed a GATE pipeline: an ordered sequence of modules, each one focused on a particular task of the whole text analysis. The pipeline was made by the following modules (which are listed in the order they were applied to the DLs):

1. Document Reset: any previous annotation is removed from the letters.
2. Tokenizer: each DL is divided into tokens. A token is a sequence of letters, a punctuation mark, a number, or a white space.
3. Lexical Lookup: each token, if it is found in any of the lexicons, is annotated with the metadata of the corresponding lexicon and entry.

4. Grammar Parser, first-level rules: some grammars are applied to identify all occurrences of diagnostic elements (regardless of negations and time). These rules exploit the metadata generated by the lexical lookup, as we said above, and by the tokenizer, which allows to identify numbers and punctuation signs.

5. Grammar Parser, second-level rules: other grammars are applied to recognize negations and time markers and to exclude from the previously found occurrences of diagnostic elements those that are negated or related to the patient's past history. The annotations produced by these grammars represent the final answers of the system: for the system, the occurrences of diagnostic elements in the DLs are those and only those that are pointed at by these second-order rules.

We developed the linguistic resources iteratively. First, we analyzed the training set to developed first-version resources. Then, we applied them to the DLs of the training set, measured the precision and recall scores they achieved, analyzed the errors they did, and refined them to reduce those errors. We repeated this cycle until we achieved satisfactory precision and recall scores on the training set.

3.5 Results Production and Quality Measurements

Once the linguistic resources and the pipeline were ready, we applied them to the test set to produce automatic annotations. Then, these automatic annotations were compared to the manual annotations produced by the cardiologists on the same test set (the gold standard), so as to measure the precision and recall scores of the system.

Precision is a measure of the capability of the system to identify only relevant portions of text (i.e., only mentions of diagnostic elements). It gives us a statistical measure of the reliability of the system (e.g., if the system says that there is an occurrence of a diagnostic element, how much can I trust it?). The precision score P is

$$P = \mathrm{TP}/(\mathrm{TP} + \mathrm{FP}). \tag{1}$$

Here, TP is the number of true positives (i.e., the system identifies a diagnostic element and the gold standard agrees) and FP is the number of false positives (i.e., the system identifies a diagnostic element, but the gold standard states the system is wrong).

Recall is a measure of the capability of the system to identify the highest possible number of relevant portions of text (i.e., all mentions of diagnostic elements). It gives us a statistical measure of the sensitivity of the system (e.g., if there are N occurrences of a diagnostic element, how many will be actually detected by the system?). The recall score R is

$$R = \mathrm{TP}/(\mathrm{TP} + \mathrm{FN}). \tag{2}$$

Here, TP is again the number of true positives and FN is the number of false negatives (i.e., the occurrences of diagnostic elements that the system failed to detect).

After calculating precision and recall, we also calculated the F-measure, i.e., the harmonic mean weighing between precision and recall, which is

$$F = 2 \times P \times R/(P + R). \tag{3}$$

On each subset of the test set, we performed two types of evaluation: by occurrence and by letter. The evaluation by occurrence is aimed at analytically measuring the performance of the system. Therefore, it takes into account the absolute number of TPs, FPs, and FNs for each diagnostic element in each DL. The evaluation by letter is aimed at measuring the performance of the system on each DL as a whole. Therefore, it assumes that a TP answer is given for a DL if and only if the DL contains at least one diagnostic element and the system correctly identifies at least one. A DL can contain in fact more than one mention of the same element. If the system examines a DL containing two mentions of the *chest pain* diagnostic element, the system will return a TP if any of the three following cases occurs (a) the system identifies both occurrences of the *chest pain* diagnostic element; (b) the system identifies only one of the two occurrences; and (c) the system identifies only one of the two occurrences or both, and it also wrongly identifies another occurrence (which would be an FP in the evaluation by occurrence). The rationale behind this more lenient evaluation is that in all three cases the system has correctly pointed out that the *chest pain* diagnostic element is mentioned in the DL.

The *by occurrence* and *by letter* evaluations have different goals: the first measures the quality of the system; the second measures its effectiveness according to its purpose in terms of quality of care. The original objective of the system, in fact, is assessing to what extent the diagnoses of AMI are supported by the identification of diagnostic elements, rather than how many times those same elements are mentioned. Therefore, we decided to evaluate the system both ways.

To perform both evaluations, we developed a dedicated software that compares the manual annotations of the gold standard with the automatic annotations of the system and then calculates precision, recall, and F-measure for both evaluations.

Table 2 shows the precision, recall, and F-measure scores obtained by the system with the different subsets of the test set.[5]

---

[5] Precision, recall, and F-measure scores were specifically calculated for each diagnostic element. We present the aggregated scores for brevity.

Table 2 System performance

Test set		Precision	Recall	F-measure
Subset 1	By occurrence	0.9157895	0.9222615	0.91901404
(AMI, from cardiology)	By letter	0.9536083	0.9438776	0.94871795
Subset 2	By occurrence	0.60294116	0.82	0.6949152
(non-AMI, from cardiology)	By letter	0.66071427	0.8604651	0.7474747
Subset 3	By occurrence	0	–	–
(non-AMI, not from cardiology)	By letter	0	–	–

4 Results

4.1 Interpretation and Discussion of Precision and Recall Scores

Three things can be noticed about the performance measures of the system reported in Table 2.

The first thing to notice is that the results of the system differ in meaning in relation to the different subsets of the test set. As regards subset 1, precision and recall scores actually describe the quality of the system and they are satisfactory. In subset 2, diagnostic elements are very rarely mentioned (only 40 mentions for all the diagnostic elements in the whole subset) and this implies that precision and recall scores are very sensitive to even few FPs or FNs. The same happens, but in an even more extreme way, with subset 3: here recall can't even be calculated—as both TPs and FNs are 0—and precision is 0 because TPs are 0 and FPs are 3 (this is hardly a surprise, given the fact that the DLs of subset 3 came from departments such as orthopedics or neurology). As regards subset 3, therefore, precision and recall scores are scarcely meaningful and we might only make a general remark about the fact that very few errors are made.

The second thing to notice is that the review of the errors of the system shows that there are three main causes for error:

1. Typos: they are frequent (e.g., *infartcion* per *infarction*) and they produce sequences of characters that the system doesn't recognize as mistyped words, thus missing to identify mentions of diagnostic elements and scoring FNs.
2. Nonstandard abbreviations and acronyms: they were not included in the lexicons and they produced more FNs.
3. Time markers of the patient's past history: some of them are beyond the capabilities of the system, which therefore scores FPs.

Other errors are due to the intrinsic ambiguity of some words or to the syntactic complexity of the text of the DLs. In general, we tried to achieve a balance between precision and recall—you reach a point where improving recall necessarily worsens precision, and vice versa—and working again on lexicons and grammars wouldn't likely improve results in a relevant measure. Instead, we think results could be improved by intervening on the writing of the DLs in three ways:

Table 3 Mentions of the diagnostic elements in the DLs

Set	At least two diagnostic elements	Less than two diagnostic elements
Test set, subset 1	121	29
Test set, subset 2	7	68
Test set, subset 3	0	75

1. Using a spell checker to reduce typos.
2. Asking doctors to avoid nonstandard abbreviations and acronyms.
3. Creating in the DL a separate field for the patient's past history.

These three interventions would ease the work of our system and enhance the exploitation of DLs for any TM or information extraction project. Moreover, they would make them more readable for human readers too.

The third thing to notice is that results are satisfactory at least for subset 1, which is composed of the DLs the system would be applied to in the real word.

4.2 System Requirements: Effectiveness and Efficiency

Let us consider now if the system might be actually used to validate diagnoses of AMI. Table 3 shows the answers of the system to the question whether the DLs mentioned two or more diagnostic elements.

We can observe that in subset 1 the system identifies 29 DLs that do not contain the mentions of at least two diagnostic elements; in subset 2, 7 DLs that contain mentions of at least two diagnostic elements; and in subset 3, no DL containing at least two diagnostic elements. Even if the answers of the system were always correct, this wouldn't mean that any of the coded diagnoses is wrong: as to the 29 DLs of subset 1, doctors might have simply recognized the diagnostic elements without mentioning them in the DL; and as to the 7 letters of subset 2, doctors might have correctly judged that the main diagnosis was not AMI. Therefore, and given the satisfactory precision and recall scores the system achieves on subset 1, we might conclude that the system has simply identified some DLs whose diagnoses of AMI might be reviewed by expert personnel (no necessarily wrong diagnosis, that's to say), automatically discarding many others that very likely don't need review. Besides, the system has identified in subset 2 some DLs with diagnoses different from AMI that might also be reviewed, though the reliability of the system, as regards subset 2, is lesser.

If we recall the system requirements we introduced above, therefore, we can make three more remarks (1) the system seems to be effective enough to support the diagnoses validation process. From a whole set of DLs with coded diagnoses of AMI or from a whole set of DLs from a cardiology department with coded diagnoses different from AMI, it might isolate a smaller subset of DLs that should actually be reviewed by expert personnel and discard the others; (2) this might make the process more efficient, because the expert personnel should not review the majority of the DLs and the processing time of the system amounts to only a few seconds (on a notebook with a 2.2 GHz processor, 150 letters are examined in about 50 s); (3) the system does not require expensive resources to work, but its development did require two valuable resources: expert personnel (two cardiologists for the annotation, a linguist to develop the linguistic resources, a computer science engineer to select the tool and develop the software for the evaluation) and time. This is nothing new, of course, and it is also obvious that these resources are profitably invested if the system can then be applied to a sufficiently high number of DLs over time without losing its effectiveness. This condition will be satisfied if the system can be effectively applied to DLs from other hospitals. Yet, if the system is applied to DLs written by doctors other than those who wrote the DLs of the training set, the system performance might worsen due to the fact that different doctors might use expressions we did not find in the original training set. We can conjecture this might happen, but we can't forecast to what extent, nor can we calculate in advance how much time it will be necessary to restore the effectiveness of the system by expanding the linguistic resources with additional training sets. Such questions can only be answered on the basis of further investigations. Yet, we believe that the issue of the robustness of the system and of its ongoing effectiveness is the most critical one. We wondered how we might face it prospectively and we conjectured that Machine Learning (ML) might be an interesting way to try both for the development and the maintenance of the system.

5 Further Developments: Machine Learning

Given our objectives, using ML means developing a system that learns to identify the mentions of diagnostic elements on the basis of a training set of DLs where mentions of diagnostic elements have been annotated as such: the system examines the annotations attached to the DLs of the training set, infer classification criteria from them, and then apply those criteria to new sets of DLs. To infer classification criteria, the system doesn't need any information other than that implied in the annotations. Yet, giving the system more information is possible and this additional information can enhance its performance. In particular, the DLs of the training set can also be annotated with lexicons and grammars. The system will use the information deriving from their metadata to refine its classification criteria. Once it has been trained, it won't need any other information to process other DLs.

To integrate ML in our system, we used the Batch Learning processing resource in GATE's Learning plug-in. We tried training the system with different combinations of annotations and for each combination we tried different learning algorithms (both a linear and a polynomial support vector machines algorithm, with τ equal to 1 or to 0.4). Then, we measured the precision, recall, and F-measure scores of the system. We won't expatiate on the scores and their discussion, but two provisional findings can be remarked:

1. More information at the time of training brings better performances.
2. If the system is trained with the annotations of the mentions of diagnostic elements, the lexical annotations, and the annotations of the tokenizer but without the annotations of the grammars, it can achieve precision scores higher than 0.9 and recall scores ranging from 0.75 to 0.87.

The first finding is what one would expect. The second finding is interesting because the development of the grammars was the most time-consuming part of the process of system development. Moreover, we conjecture that grammars are the least robust resource. Therefore, the possibility of achieving good results without using deterministic grammars is noteworthy. Combining specialized lexicons and an ML system might grant good results in terms of effectiveness, robustness, and efficiency of development and maintenance.

Acknowledgments The project was realized by the authors and the following people: Pietro Barbieri, M.D. (Azienda Ospedaliera di Melegnano), developed the overall design and acted as a domain expert (cardiology); Barbara Severgnini, M.D. (Azienda Ospedaliera di Melegnano), also acted as a domain expert (cardiology); Mauro Maistrello, M.D. (Azienda Ospedaliera di Melegnano), extracted the DLs from the hospitals' databases and anonymized them; and professor Anna Maria Paganoni (Politecnico di Milano, Maths Department "Francesco Brioschi") and engineer Lorenzo Vayno (Politecnico di Milano) experimented with ML methods.

References

1. Feldman, R., Sanger, J.: The Text Mining Handbook. Advanced Approaches in Analyzing Unstructured Data. Cambridge University Press, New York, NY (2007)
2. Warrer, P., Hansen, E.H., Juhl-Jensen, L., Aagaard, L.: Using text-mining techniques in electronic patient records to identify ADRs from medicine use. Br. J. Clin. Pharmacol. **73**(5), 674–684 (2012). doi:10.1111/j.1365-2125.2011.04153.x
3. Penz, J.F., Wilcox, A.B.., Hurdle, J.F.: Automated identification of adverse events related to central venous catheters. J. Biomed. Inform. **40**(2), 174–182 (2007). doi:10.1016/j.jbi.2006.06.003
4. Lakhani, P., Kim, W., Langlotz, C.P.: Automated detection of critical results in radiology reports. J. Digit. Imaging **25**(1), 30–36 (2012). doi:10.1007/s10278-011-9426-6
5. He, Q., Veldkamp, B.P., de Vries, T.: Screening for posttraumatic stress disorder using verbal features in self narratives: A text mining approach. Psychiatry Res. (2012). doi:10.1016/j.psychres.2012.01.032
6. Cunningham, H. et al.: Text Processing with GATE (Version 6). University of Sheffield, Department of Computer Science (2011)
7. Ananiadou, S., McNaught, J.: Text Mining for Biology and Biomedicine. Artech House, Boston/London (2006)

Part II
New Diagnostic and Therapeutic Strategies in ACS

PREDESTINATION: PRimary vEntricular fibrillation and suDden dEath during a firST myocardIal iNfArcTION: Genetic Basis

Gaetano M. De Ferrari, Valentina De Regibus, Vincenzo Gionti, Daniela Civardi, Roberto Insolia, Matteo Pedrazzini, Davide Gentilini, Annamaria Di Blasio, Lia Crotti, and Peter J. Schwartz

G.M. De Ferrari • D. Civardi • M. Pedrazzini
Department of Cardiology, Fondazione IRCCS Policlinico S. Matteo, Pavia, Italy
e-mail: g.deferrari@smatteo.pv.it; studio.predestination@gmail.com; m.pedrazzini@smatteo.pv.it

V. De Regibus • V. Gionti
Department of Cardiology, Fondazione IRCCS Policlinico S. Matteo, Pavia, Italy

Department of Molecular Medicine, Unit of Cardiology, University of Pavia, Pavia, Italy
e-mail: valentina.deregibus@gmail.com; vincenzo.gionti@libero.it

R. Insolia
Department of Molecular Medicine, Unit of Cardiology, University of Pavia, Pavia, Italy
e-mail: r.insolia@smatteo.pv.it

D. Gentilini • A. Di Blasio
Molecular Biology Laboratory, Istituto Auxologico Italiano IRCCS, Milan, Italy
e-mail: gentilini.davide@gmail.com; a.diblasio@auxologico.it

L. Crotti
Department of Cardiology, Fondazione IRCCS Policlinico S. Matteo, Pavia, Italy

Department of Molecular Medicine, Unit of Cardiology, University of Pavia, Pavia, Italy

Institute of Human Genetics, Helmholtz Zentrum Muenchen, Neuherberg, Germany
e-mail: liacrotti@yahoo.it

P.J. Schwartz (✉)
Department of Cardiology, Fondazione IRCCS Policlinico S. Matteo, Pavia, Italy

Department of Molecular Medicine, Unit of Cardiology, University of Pavia, Pavia, Italy

Department of Internal Medicine, University of Stellenbosch, Stellenbosch, South Africa

Department of Medicine, Cardiovascular Genetics Laboratory, Hatter Institute for Cardiovascular Research in Africa, University of Cape Town, Cape Town, South Africa
e-mail: peter.schwartz@unipv.it

N. Grieco et al. (eds.), *New Diagnostic, Therapeutic and Organizational Strategies for Acute Coronary Syndromes Patients*, Contributions to Statistics,
DOI 10.1007/978-88-470-5379-3_6, © Springer-Verlag Italia 2013

Abstract Sudden cardiac death (SCD) is the leading cause of death in the age group 20–65 years, in the western world, with an enormous social and economic impact. The majority of the cases of ventricular fibrillation (VF) occur in patients without a preexisting structural heart disease and represent the first manifestation of coronary artery disease. In most of these cases, VF occurs in the early phase of myocardial infarction (MI) and it is then called primary VF. Although several factors have been associated in various studies with primary VF a recent meta-analysis found no evidence for risk factors other than ST elevation and time from onset of symptoms.

In the past several years, few studies have found that a family history of sudden cardiac death (SCD) is a risk factor for primary VF suggesting that this dramatic event may be favored by the genetic background. To explore this possibility we designed the ongoing PREDESTINATION Study, enrolling subjects under 75 years of age with a first MI complicated by primary VF and a control group of subjects with a first uncomplicated MI.

Data so far available confirm the association between a family history of SCD and primary VF and suggest that hypokalemia and prolonged QT interval may favor its occurrence. The genetic analysis has already provided some interesting suggestions that will need to be confirmed by the continuation of the enrolment and joint analysis with data deriving from similar patient populations.

1 Background

Sudden cardiac death (SCD) is the leading cause of death in the age group 20–65 years, in the western world, with an enormous social and economic impact. According to the Maastricht Study, the incidence of SCD in the age group 20–75 years is 5:10,000/year [1]. In most cases SCD is due to ventricular fibrillation (VF). Even though VF may often occur in the setting of a significant underlying heart disease such as a previous myocardial infarction (MI) or heart failure, the majority of cases of VF occur in patients without a preexisting structural heart disease and represent the first manifestation of coronary artery disease. In most of these cases, VF occurs in the early phase of MI and it is then called primary VF. Primary VF accounts for approximately one third of all cases of SCD.

Several factors have been associated in various studies with primary VF including younger age, male gender, smoking, absence of history of diabetes, lower serum potassium concentration, and inferior wall infarct location, but these findings have not been reproducible [2]. Indeed, a meta-analysis including over 50,000 patients with acute MI found no evidence for risk factors for primary VF other than ST elevation and time from onset of symptoms [2].

Friedlander et al. have examined whether family history of myocardial infarction or primary cardiac arrest was a risk factor for primary cardiac arrest (CA) [3]. They enrolled subjects suffering primary CA, defined as a cardiac arrest that was a result of heart disease and not "secondary" to trauma, drug overdose, respiratory failure, renal failure, end-stage liver disease, cancer, or other noncardiac causes. As control group they enrolled healthy volunteers identified from the community. A history of MI/primary CA among first-degree relatives of cardiac arrest patients was almost 50 % higher than that in first-degree relatives of control subjects. In a multivariate logistic model, family history of MI/primary CA was associated with primary CA (OR 1.58; 95 % CI: 1.29–1.95) even after adjustment for other common risk factors. A major limitation of this study is that the control group consisted of healthy subjects without a history of cardiovascular disease.

Further studies provided strong evidence that a familial history of sudden cardiac death could be associated to primary VF. The "Paris Prospective Study" first showed that a family history of sudden death (SD) is an independent risk factor of SD [4]. The study enrolled 7,079 men employed by the Paris Civil Service from 1967 to 1972. During a follow-up of 23 years, 118 subjects died suddenly (sudden death was defined as a natural death occurring within 1 h of onset of acute symptoms) and 192 had a fatal myocardial infarction (death strictly related to myocardial infarction). The authors found that a parental history of sudden death was a risk factor of sudden death (RR, 1.95; 95 % CI: 1.23–3.10), but was not associated with the occurrence of fatal myocardial infarction (RR, 0.97; 95 % CI: 0.60–1.55). Also in multivariate analysis including other cardiovascular risk factors, family history of sudden death (SD) proved to be an independent risk factor of SD (RR, 1.80; 95 % CI: 1.11–2.88), but not of fatal MI (RR, 0.85; 95 % CI: 0.52–1.39). The subjects with a history of SD in both parents had a sudden death RR of 9.44.

Other two important clinical studies supported these data. Dekker et al. found that among subjects with a first MI, the presence of SCD among first-degree relatives was a strong predictor for primary VF [5]. They enrolled 330 survivors of primary VF and 372 controls who suffered a first myocardial infarction. They found that 43.1 % of survivors of primary VF had 1 or more cases of sudden death among parents and siblings while only 25.1 % of controls had this familiarity. Likewise, aborted sudden death among parents and siblings occurred in 3.8 % of cases and 1.5 % of controls. SCD among parents and siblings significantly increased the risk of primary VF (OR 2.72). A familial history of SCD remained a risk factor for primary VF also in a multivariable model (3.30; 95 % CI: 1.91–5.68).

Kaikkonnen et al. have investigated the family history of sudden death among victims of SCD, survivors of acute myocardial infarction, and healthy control subjects [6]. The occurrence of SCD among first-degree relatives of SCD victims was significantly higher than among first-degree relatives of MI survivors (OR 1.6; 95 % CI: 1.2–2.2; $P = 0.01$) and than among first-degree relatives of control subjects (OR 2.2; 95 % CI: 1.6–3.0; $P = 0.001$). This study confirmed that history of SCD in more than 1 first-degree relatives increase the risk of SCD (OR 3.3. 95 % CI, 1.4–7.8; $P = 0.01$). Compared to the control group, a family history of SCD is 11.3 times more frequent in SCD victims (OR 11.3; 95 % CI, 4.0–31.8; $P < 0.001$).

Overall, the studies presented above strongly suggest that primary VF may be favored by the genetic background. However, the genetic markers associated to primary VF are still unknown. In order to increase our understanding on the potential genetic influence on primary VF, specifically designed studies must be carried out comparing patients with this event with appropriate controls. To increase the reliability of the findings, it is very important to define a clear phenotype characterizing patients to be enrolled. It is with this purpose that we designed the PREDESTINATION Study.

2 PREDESTINATION: Study Design

PREDESTINATION (**PR**imary v**E**ntricular fibrillation and su**D**den d**E**ath during a fir**ST** myocard**I**al i**Nf**Arc**TION**: genetic basis) is an ongoing case–control study aiming to identify common genetic variants, clinical and epidemiological features that increase the risk of primary VF. The primary aim of the study is to identify the "genetic make-up" likely to be associated to the development of VF during myocardial infarction. The secondary goal is to increase knowledge of clinical epidemiological factors that may facilitate the onset of primary VF and analyze their interaction with genetic background.

2.1 *Population*

The study involved the enrollment of subjects under 75 years of age with a first MI complicated by primary VF (cases) and a control group of subjects with a first uncomplicated MI (controls). Each case was matched with 3 controls according to age ($\pm$ 5 year), gender, and type of MI (anterior ST elevation, not-anterior ST elevation, or non-ST elevation MI). The patients could qualify as a case if the arrhythmia was documented by an ECG performed and if it occurred before myocardial revascularization and within 24 h from symptom onset.

We excluded subjects with >75 years, subjects with a previous MI or ventricular dysfunction, and subjects with diseases that could favor the onset of VF, such as long QT syndrome, arrhythmogenic right ventricular cardiomyopathy, and hypertrophic cardiomyopathy.

We enrolled a third group of subjects under 75 years old, who underwent at least three uncomplicated MI (super controls). We decided to study this population with the purpose of searching the presence of potential protective factors.

Case Report Form

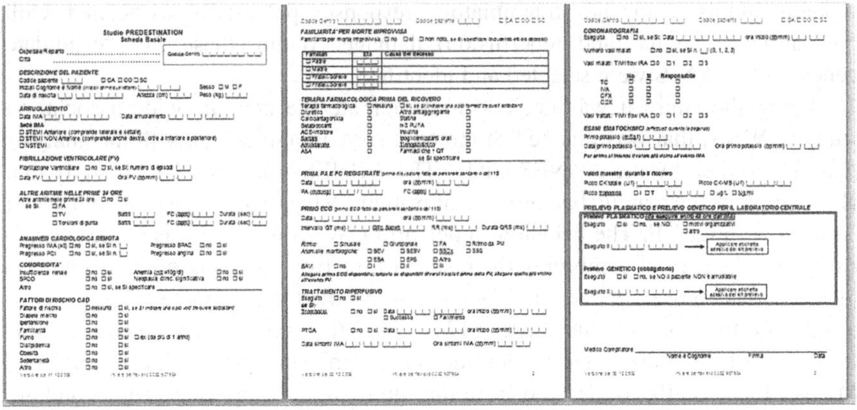

Fig. 1 Case report form used to collect the data

2.2 Clinical Data Collection

For each subject enrolled the following information was collected:

- Baseline characteristics: cardiovascular risk factors, prior cardiovascular events, family history of sudden death, and previous therapy.
- Myocardial infarction characteristics: date and hour of MI, site of MI, occurrence of VF, and other arrhythmia during the first 24 h.
- ECG characteristics.
- Type and timing of cardiac revascularization.
- Blood tests.

All these data were collected in a "case report form" (shown in Fig. 1).

2.3 Genetic Analysis

All subjects enrolled in the study underwent peripheral venipuncture for blood sampling and subsequent extraction of genomic DNA. The DNA extraction (Maxwell® 16 System DNA Purification Kits) was performed from the blood sample with a semiautomated method, through cell lysis, DNA binding to magnetic beads, and final elution in a suitable buffer. We first performed a medium-density genotyping of the enrolled population, using a custom set of 1,536 bend chip SNPs (single-nucleotide polymorphism), through GoldenGate Assay (Illumina) with an approach of "candidate gene." For this purpose we have carefully selected 219 genes, including those coding for cardiac ion channels and for molecules involved both in the neural control of the heart (adrenergic cascade and renin–angiotensin–aldosterone system) and in arrhythmic pathologies as well as proteins involved in the inflammatory response, potentially associated with myocardial ischemia (and reperfusion) damage. Within these 219 "candidate genes," 1,536 SNPs were selected and identified.

During the study it was decided to anticipate the genome-wide association study (GWAS) that was planned as the next step, in agreement with the analysis plan undertaken by the AGNES study. The AGNES study is a Dutch study that also compares the genetic background of primary VF patients to that of control MI patients without VF. The decision to perform GWAS directly was made specifically with the idea of combining the results of the two studies in order to increase the statistical power of the findings. We performed the genome-wide analysis using Illumina HumanOmniExpress-12 v.1 chip that allows simultaneous review of a total of 770,000 single-nucleotide polymorphisms (SNPs) for 12 subjects. Most of these SNPs are derived from the International Hap Map Project and are therefore SNPs markers since their genotyping also allows to know the genotype of other SNPs adjacent thereto. The use of these SNPs markers therefore confers a broader coverage of the genome that, with the chip used in this study, reaches 95 %.

Before carrying out the association analysis, an extensive quality control was performed both on the subjects enrolled and the markers genotyped. Per-individual QC consisted of four steps (1) identification of individuals with discordant sex information, (2) identification of individuals with outlying missing genotype or heterozygosity rates, (3) identification of duplicated or related individuals, and (4) identification of individuals of divergent ancestry. This last step was performed using the EIGENSTRAT software for the Principal Component Analysis. This kind of analysis provides information on the genetic background of the population studied that can be used as covariates in the logistic regression. The correction of a candidate marker's variation in frequency across ancestral populations allows minimizing spurious associations, thus maximizing power to detect true associations. Per-marker QC was performed according to the following steps (a) identification of SNPs with an excessive missing genotype, (b) identification of SNPs showing a significant deviation from Hardy–Weinberg equilibrium (HWE), (c) identification of SNPs with significantly different missing genotype rates between cases and controls, and (d) the removal of all markers with a very low minor allele frequency (MAF).

2.4 Statistical Analysis

In the present report data are presented as mean ± SD. Contingency tables were used to derive chi-square values and associated OR for the association between epidemiological and clinical characteristics and the occurrence of VF.

Fig. 2 Family history of
SCD among first-degree
relatives was present in 12 %
of cases and in 6 % of controls

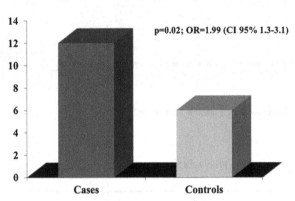

Prevalence of Family History of SCD

p=0.02; OR=1.99 (CI 95% 1.3-3.1)

3   Results and Discussion

3.1   Epidemiological Data

So far, 812 patients have been enrolled. Statistical analysis was performed on the clinical and epidemiological characteristics of the first 206 cases and 414 controls. The mean age of the population was 58 ± 10 years and 15 % of the subjects are female. Among the cases 54 % of the subjects had an anterior MI, and control subjects were matched to the site of MI.

The ongoing analysis on the epidemiological characteristics show that a family history of SCD among first-degree relatives was present in 12 % of cases and in 6 % of controls (OR 1.99; 95 % CI: 1.3–3.1; $P = 0.02$; see Fig. 2).

These data are consistent with the findings of the studies by Dekker and Kaikkonnen, as detailed in Fig. 3, which shows our findings relative to those of these studies.

For each participant we collected the first ECG recorded by the emergency medical system; in particular for cases we collected the ECG temporally closer to the episode of VF. We analyzed morphologic characteristics, like PQ, QRS, QT intervals, conduction disorders, and rhythm disorders.

So far, interesting results have emerged from the analysis of the QT interval. We evaluated the correct QT interval (QTc) calculated with the Bazett formula. The average QTc in cases was 416 ± 51 ms and the average QTc in controls was 411 ± 43 ms. This difference in average QTc between the two groups was not statistically significant ($P = 0.32$). However, a prolonged QT interval, defined as QTc > 440 ms, was present in 32 % of cases and in 22 % of controls (OR 1.6; 95 % CI: 1.2–2.2; $P = 0.01$). This suggests that subjects with a prolonged QTc during the early phases of the MI had a 1.6 greater risk of developing a VF compared with subjects with QTc $\leq$ 440 ms. This finding is in agreement with previous studies indicating higher mortality among patients with a prolonged QT interval after MI [7].

Family History of SCD as a Predictor of Primary VF in Case-Control Studies

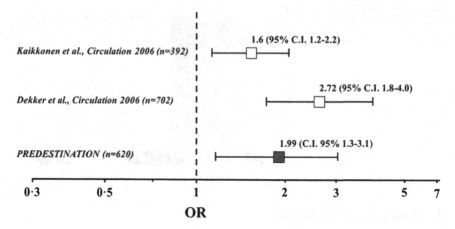

Fig. 3 Figure comparing data showed in Fig. 2 with the findings of the studies by Dekker [5] and Kaikkonnen[6]. The consistency of the results is evident

Serum potassium values were evaluated as soon as possible after hospital admission (among cases this was often after the occurrence of VF). The average value of plasma potassium was 3.7 ± 0.5 mEq/l in cases and 3.9 ± 0.5 mEq/l in controls ($p < 0.0001$). Moreover, hypokalemia (defined as $K < 3.5$ mEq) was present in 31 % of cases and in 13 % of controls, so that the occurrence of primary VF in subjects with a low plasma potassium was nearly three times greater compared with subjects with a normal potassium (OR 3.1; 95 % CI: 2.0–4.9; $p < 0.0001$).

Several studies have demonstrated an association between hypokalemia and ventricular arrhythmias during acute MI [8–10]. The main reason for hypokalemia in the early phase of an acute myocardial infarction is most likely an activation of the sympathetic nervous system leading to an influx of potassium from the extracellular to the intracellular body fluid compartment. A limitation of our study, as mentioned above, is the fact that most of the cases enrolled had an out-of-hospital VF so that the value of plasma potassium value is measured after the arrhythmia.

3.2 Preliminary Results of Genetic Analysis

3.2.1 Candidate Gene Approach

As first step of the analysis, we applied a candidate gene approach. For this purpose, we tested 319 samples (101 cases and 218 controls) using the custom-made chip (Illumina). Overall, 16 polymorphisms have been identified, relating to 12 different genes, whose association with the risk of VF was statistically significant in univariate analysis but did not reach conventional statistical significance due to the necessary correction of p value for multiple comparisons.

The results related to genes coding for angiotensin converting enzyme I (ACE), for the angiotensin II type 1 receptor (AGTR1), and genes related to caveolin appear particularly promising given their potential involvement in the regulation of ion channels and the finding of a greater likelihood on QT prolongation among patients with VF.

To this regard, some speculative hypotheses may be suggested. It is known that the renin–angiotensin system may potentially favor the occurrence of arrhythmias through two distinct mechanisms. RAAS can interact with mechanisms of intracellular calcium release, through the activation of the L-type calcium channels [11–13]. Additionally, the renin–angiotensin system may promote the development of malignant ventricular arrhythmias through a reduction of I_{Kr}, which is a potassium repolarizing current [14]. Both electrophysiological mechanisms may lead to a prolongation of action potential duration which manifests on the surface ECG as a prolongation of the QT interval. Caveolin is a protein involved in the cellular signaling. In the heart, caveolin is associated with several proteins including Nav1.5 [15], Kv1.5, HCN4 [16], Na/Ca exchanger [17], IP3 receptor [18], TRP channels [19], Cav1.2, and PMCA [20]. Mutations in the gene for caveolin 3 and overexpression of Nav1.5 are associated with increase in persistent (late) sodium current, as found in LQT3 [21]. Caveolin mutations are also present in LQT9. These findings suggest a potential role of caveolin in the development of ventricular arrhythmias, which will need to be further evaluated.

Among other genes that we had focused our attention on, there is NOS1AP. We have previously demonstrated that polymorphisms in NOS1AP, known to be associated with QT interval duration, are linked to an increased risk of life-threatening arrhythmias in patients with LQT1 [22]. Conflicting data exist regarding the role of NOS1AP in the risk of SCD [23–25]. We were therefore interested in assessing the possible presence of an association between NOS1AP polymorphism and primary VF. Our preliminary data do not suggest that this correlation is present.

3.2.2 Genome-Wide Approach

As second step we performed a genome-wide association study in 576 subjects. The results of quality control have led to the elimination of genotyped 29 individuals, obtaining a final sample of 547 subjects of which 210 are cases and 337 are controls. A total of 630,709 SNPs have passed the quality control and were therefore used for the analysis of association performed by the software Plink.

The genome-wide association study performed in the AGNES study showed a statistically significant association to VF at 21q21 (rs2824292, OR 1.78; 95 % CI: 1.47–2.13; $P = 3.3 \times 10^{-10}$) [26]. The closest gene to this SNP is CXADR, which encodes a viral receptor previously implicated in myocarditis and dilated cardiomyopathy [27, 28] and which has been also identified as a modulator of cardiac conduction [29, 30]. However, our preliminary analysis did not confirm so far this strong association.

3.3 Conclusions

The preliminary data from the ongoing case–control study PREDESTINATION suggest that some clinical characteristics such as hypokalemia and prolonged QT interval may favor the occurrence of ventricular fibrillation during acute myocardial infarction. Furthermore the findings so far are in good agreement with the concept that primary ventricular fibrillation may have a familiar basis. The genetic analysis is also only preliminary but has provided some interesting suggestions. Completion of the analysis and combination of the data with the similar study AGNES will reveal whether indeed new markers for an increased likelihood of ventricular fibrillation during myocardial infarction will become available and will increase our understanding of the pathophysiology of sudden cardiac death.

Acknowledgments We thank Pinuccia De Tomasi, BS, for the expert editorial support.

References

1. De Vreede-Swagemakers, J.J., Gorgels, A.P., Dubois-Arbouw, W.I., Van Ree, J.W., Daemen, M.J., Houben, L.G., Wellens, H.J.: Out-of-hospital cardiac arrest in the 1990's: a population-based study in the Maastricht area on incidence, characteristics and survival. J. Am. Coll. Cardiol. **30**, 1500–1505 (1997)
2. Gheeraert, P.J., De Buyzere, M.L., Taeymans, Y.M., Gillebert, T.C., Henriques, J.P., De Backer, G., De Bacquer, D.: Risk factors for primary ventricular fibrillation during acute myocardial infarction: a systematic review and meta-analysis. Eur. Heart J. **27**, 2499–2510 (2006)
3. Friedlander, Y., Siscovick, D.S., Weinmann, S., Austin, M.A., Psaty, B.M., Lemaitre, R.N., Arbogast, P., Raghunathan, T.E., Cobb, L.A.: Family history as a risk factor for primary cardiac arrest. Circulation **97**, 155–160 (1998)
4. Jouven, X., Desnos, M., Guerot, C., Ducimetière, P.: Predicting sudden death in the population: the Paris prospective study I. Circulation **99**, 1978–1983 (1999)
5. Dekker, L.R., Bezzina, C.R., Henriques, J.P., Tanck, M.W., Koch, K.T., Alings, M.W., Arnold, A.E., de Boer, M.J., Gorgels, A.P., Michels, H.R., Verkerk, A., Verheugt, F.W., Zijlstra, F., Wilde, A.A.: Familial sudden death is an important risk factor for primary ventricular fibrillation: a case–control study in acute myocardial infarction patients. Circulation **114**, 1140–1145 (2006)
6. Kaikkonen, K.S., Kortelainen, M.L., Linna, E., Huikuri, H.V.: Family history and the risk of sudden cardiac death as a manifestation of an acute coronary event. Circulation **114**, 1462–1467 (2006)
7. Schwartz, P.J., Wolf, S.: QT interval prolongation as predictor of sudden death in patients with myocardial infarction. Circulation **57**, 1074–1077 (1978)
8. Clausen, T.G., Brocks, K., Ibsen, H.: Hypokalemia and ventricular arrhythmias in acute myocardial infarction. Acta Med. Scand. **224**, 531–537 (1988)
9. Nordrehaug, J.E., von der Lippe, G.: Hypokalaemia and ventricular fibrillation in acute myocardial infarction. Br. Heart J. **50**, 525–529 (1983)

10. Nordrehaug, J.E., Johannessen, K.A., von der Lippe, G.: Serum potassium concentration as a risk factor of ventricular arrhythmias early in acute myocardial infarction. Circulation **71**, 645–649 (1985)

11. Krizanova, O., Orlicky, J., Masanova, C.S., Juhaszova, M., Hudecova, S.: Angiotensin I modulates Ca-transport systems in the rat heart through angiotensin II. J. Mol. Cell. Cardiol. **29**, 1739–1746 (1997)

12. Harada, K., Komuro, I., Hayashi, D., Sugaya, T., Murakami, K., Yazaki, Y.: Angiotensin II type 1a receptor is involved in the occurrence of reperfusion arrhythmias. Circulation **97**, 315–317 (1998)

13. Ozer, M.K., Sahna, E., Birincioglu, M., Acet, A.: Effects of captopril and losartan on myocardial ischemia-reperfusion induced arrhythmias and necrosis in rats. Pharmacol. Res. **45**, 257–263 (2002)

14. Wang, Y.H., Shi, C.X., Dong, F., Sheng, J.W., Xu, Y.F.: Inhibition of the rapid component of the delayed rectifier potassium current in ventricular myocytes by angiotensin II via the AT1 receptor. Br. J. Pharmacol. **154**, 429–439 (2008)

15. Yarbrough, T.L., Lu, T., Lee, H.C., Shibata, E.F.: Localization of cardiac sodium channels in caveolin-rich membrane domains: regulation of sodium current amplitude. Circ. Res. **90**, 443–449 (2002)

16. Barbuti, A., Gravante, B., Riolfo, M., Milanesi, R., Terragni, B., DiFrancesco, D.: Localization of pacemaker channels in lipid rafts regulates channel kinetics. Circ. Res. **94**, 1325–1331 (2004)

17. Bossuyt, J., Taylor, B.E., James-Kracke, M., Hale, C.C.: The cardiac sodium-calcium exchanger associates with caveolin-3. Ann. N. Y. Acad. Sci. **976**, 197–204 (2002)

18. Fujimoto, T., Nakade, S., Miyawaki, A., Mikoshiba, K., Ogawa, K.: Localization of inositol 1,4,5-trisphosphate receptor-like protein in plasmalemmal caveolae. J. Cell Biol. **119**, 1507–1513 (1992)

19. Lockwich, T.P., Liu, X., Singh, B.B., Jadlowiec, J., Weiland, S., Ambudkar, I.S.: Assembly of Trp1 in a signaling complex associated with caveolin-scaffolding lipid raft domains. J. Biol. Chem. **275**, 11934–11942 (2000)

20. Fujimoto, T.: Calcium pump of the plasma membrane is localized in caveolae. J. Cell Biol. **120**, 1147–1157 (1993)

21. Vatta, M., Ackerman, M.J., Ye, B., Makielski, J.C., Ughanze, E.E., Taylor, E.W., Tester, D.J., Balijepalli, R.C., Foell, J.D., Li, Z., Kamp, T.J., Towbin, J.A.: Mutant caveolin-3 induces persistent late sodium current and is associated with long-QT syndrome. Circulation **114**, 2104–2112 (2006)

22. Crotti, L., Monti, M.C., Insolia, R., Peljto, A., Goosen, A., Brink, P.A., Greenberg, D.A., Schwartz, P.J., George Jr., A.L.: NOS1AP is a genetic modifier of the long-QT syndrome. Circulation **120**, 1657–1663 (2009)

23. Kao, W.H., Arking, D.E., Post, W., Rea, T.D., Sotoodehnia, N., Prineas, R.J., Bishe, B., Doan, B.Q., Boerwinkle, E., Psaty, B.M., Tomaselli, G.F., Coresh, J., Siscovick, D.S., Marbán, E., Spooner, P.M., Burke, G.L., Chakravarti, A.: Genetic variations in nitric oxide synthase 1 adaptor protein are associated with sudden cardiac death in US white community-based populations. Circulation **119**, 940–951 (2009)

24. Newton-Cheh, C., Guo, C.Y., Wang, T.J., O'Donnell, C.J., Levy, D., Larson, M.G.: Genome-wide association study of electrocardiographic and heart rate variability traits: the Framingham Heart Study. BMC Med. Genet. **8**(Suppl 1), S7 (2007)

25. Pfeufer, A., Sanna, S., Arking, D.E., Müller, M., Gateva, V., Fuchsberger, C., Ehret, G.B., Orrú, M., Pattaro, C., Köttgen, A., Perz, S., Usala, G., Barbalic, M., Li, M., Pütz, B., Scuteri, A., Prineas, R.J., Sinner, M.F., Gieger, C., Najjar, S.S., Kao, W.H., Mühleisen, T.W., Dei, M., Happle, C., Möhlenkamp, S., Crisponi, L., Erbel, R., Jöckel, K.H., Naitza, S., Steinbeck, G., Marroni, F., Hicks, A.A., Lakatta, E., Müller-Myhsok, B., Pramstaller, P.P., Wichmann, H.E., Schlessinger, D., Boerwinkle, E., Meitinger, T., Uda, M., Coresh, J., Kääb, S., Abecasis, G.R.,

Chakravarti, A.: Common variants at ten loci modulate the QT interval duration in the QTSCD Study. Nat. Genet. **41**, 407–414 (2009)
26. Bezzina, C.R., Pazoki, R., Bardai, A., Marsman, R.F., de Jong, J.S., Blom, M.T., Scicluna, B. P., Jukema, J.W., Bindraban, N.R., Lichtner, P., Pfeufer, A., Bishopric, N.H., Roden, D.M., Meitinger, T., Chugh, S.S., Myerburg, R.J., Jouven, X., Kääb, S., Dekker, L.R., Tan, H.L., Tanck, M.W., Wilde, A.A.: Genome-wide association study identifies a susceptibility locus at 21q21 for ventricular fibrillation in acute myocardial infarction. Nat. Genet. **42**, 688–691 (2010)
27. Bowles, N.E., Richardson, P.J., Olsen, E.G., Archard, L.C.: Detection of Coxsackie-B-virus-specific RNA sequences in myocardial biopsy samples from patients with myocarditis and dilated cardiomyopathy. Lancet **1**, 1120–1123 (1986)
28. Pauschinger, M., Bowles, N.E., Fuentes-Garcia, F.J., Pham, V., Kühl, U., Schwimmbeck, P.L., Schultheiss, H.P., Towbin, J.A.: Detection of adenoviral genome in the myocardium of adult patients with idiopathic left ventricular dysfunction. Circulation **99**, 1348–1354 (1999)
29. Lisewski, U., Shi, Y., Wrackmeyer, U., Fischer, R., Chen, C., Schirdewan, A., Jüttner, R., Rathjen, F., Poller, W., Radke, M.H., Gotthardt, M.: The tight junction protein CAR regulates cardiac conduction and cell-cell communication. J. Exp. Med. **205**, 2369–2379 (2008)
30. Lim, B.K., Xiong, D., Dorner, A., Youn, T.J., Yung, A., Liu, T.I., Gu, Y., Dalton, N.D., Wright, A.T., Evans, S.M., Chen, J., Peterson, K.L., McCulloch, A.D., Yajima, T., Knowlton, K.U.: Coxsackievirus and adenovirus receptor (CAR) mediates atrioventricular-node function and connexin 45 localization in the murine heart. J. Clin. Invest. **118**, 2758–2770 (2008)

MicroRNAs and Tissue Response to Acute Ischemia

Pasquale Fasanaro and Fabio Martelli

Abstract MicroRNAs (miRNAs) are 21–23-nucleotide non-protein-coding RNA molecules that act as negative regulators of gene expression, modulating the stability and/or the translational efficiency of target messenger RNAs. This chapter describes miRNA regulation and function in tissue response to acute ischemia, focusing on miRNAs role in acute myocardial infarction. The role played by specific miRNAs in the regulation of apoptosis, fibrosis, regeneration, and myocardial arrhythmias is illustrated. Examples of the miRNA involvement in noncardiac ischemia are also included. The identification of specific miRNAs as key regulators of the response to ischemia has opened new clinical avenues. miRNAs may constitute excellent noninvasive disease biomarkers. Furthermore, innovative strategies targeting miRNAs, aimed at reducing the levels of pathogenic or aberrantly expressed miRNAs or to elevate the levels of miRNAs with beneficial functions, have been developed and could be applied in the treatment of ischemic diseases. The efficacy of these strategies is confirmed by two paradigmatic reports in which miRNAs have been targeted to improve cardiac function in preclinical models of myocardial infarction. Specifically, miR-210 upregulation and miR-15 inhibition can both protect against cardiac injury and rescue cardiac function after myocardial infarction.

P. Fasanaro
Vascular Pathology Laboratory, Istituto Dermopatico dell'Immacolata – IRCCS, Rome, Italy
e-mail: p.fasanaro@gmail.com

F. Martelli (✉)
Molecular Cardiology Laboratory, IRCCS Policlinico San Donato, San Donato Milanese, Milan, Italy
e-mail: fabio.martelli@grupposandonato.it

N. Grieco et al. (eds.), *New Diagnostic, Therapeutic and Organizational Strategies for Acute Coronary Syndromes Patients*, Contributions to Statistics,
DOI 10.1007/978-88-470-5379-3_7, © Springer-Verlag Italia 2013

1 MicroRNAs

MicroRNAs (miRNAs) are 21–23-nucleotide non-protein-coding RNA molecules that act as negative regulators of gene expression, modulating the translational efficiency and/or the stability of target messenger RNAs [1–3]. After the discovery of the first two miRNAs, lin-4 and let-7, that control key steps in Caenorhabditis elegans development, hundreds of miRNAs have been identified by molecular cloning and bioinformatics approaches. miRNA activity is involved in the control of a wide range of biological functions and processes, such as development, differentiation, metabolism, growth, proliferation, and apoptosis [4]. While most authors observed a repressive role of miRNAs, few opposite examples have been described as well [5]. To date, more than 2,000 human miRNAs have been cloned, and the progressive improvement of target prediction tools indicates an ever-increasing portion of protein-coding genes as miRNA controlled. Different tissues and physiological conditions are each associated to a specific pattern of miRNA expression (miRNA signatures), and altered miRNA signatures have been associated to specific diseases. Bartel's group estimated that more than 45,000 miRNA target sites within human 3′UTRs display higher conservation than expected for randomly selected sequences and that more than 60 % of human protein-coding genes have been under selective pressure to maintain pairing to miRNAs [6]. In this scenario, it may prove difficult to find a biological process or function that is not at least in certain aspects under the influence of miRNAs. Moreover, considering that a single miRNA may target multiple transcripts and that individual transcripts may be subject to regulation by multiple miRNAs, the complexity of the scenario of miRNA-dependent regulation of gene expression is constantly rising.

1.1 *miRNA Biogenesis*

miRNA genes can be expressed as independent transcripts, can be included in polycistronic transcripts that often encode multiple miRNAs, or can be embedded in the introns of protein-coding genes. The biogenesis of an miRNA (Fig. 1) begins with a primary transcript, termed the pri-miRNA, generally transcribed by RNA polymerase II, albeit certain miRNAs are RNA polymerase III transcribed (see [2, 7, 8] for extensive reviews on regulation of microRNA biogenesis, function, and decay). The pri-miRNA, which may be thousands of nucleotides long, contains the active miRNA in a stem–loop structure. This hairpin undergoes nuclear cleavage by the ribonuclease III Drosha complexed to the RNA-binding protein DGCR8/Pasha to generate a 70–100 nucleotide hairpin-shaped pre-miRNA. It is worth noting that most intronic miRNAs can be processed from unspliced intronic regions before splicing catalysis; however, there is a subset of intronic miRNAs, named mirtrons, that enters in the miRNA-processing pathway without Drosha-mediated cleavage

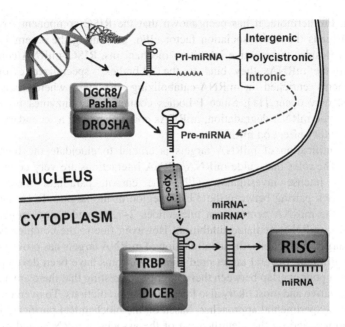

Fig. 1 miRNA biogenesis. miRNAs are expressed independently, included in polycistronic transcripts or embedded in the introns of mRNAs. The pri-miRNA is cleaved in the nucleus by the complex Drosha/DGCR8 to generate a 70–100 nucleotide long hairpin-shaped pre-miRNA. Some intronic pri-miRNAs enter in the miRNA-processing pathway without Drosha-mediated cleavage. The pre-miRNA is shuttled to the cytoplasm by Exportin 5 (Xpo-5) and further processed by the ribonuclease III Dicer, complexed to TRBP (TAR RNA-binding protein), forming the mature 22-nt miRNA:miRNA* duplex. While the strand miRNA* is typically degraded, the mature single-stranded miRNA is incorporated into the RISC complex

[9]. The pre-miRNA is transported to the cytoplasm by the nuclear export factor Exportin-5 (Xpo-5) and further processed by the ribonuclease III Dicer, complexed to TRBP (TAR RNA-binding protein), to form the mature 22-nt miRNA:miRNA* duplex. The complementary strand miRNA* is typically degraded, while the mature single-stranded form is incorporated into the RNA-induced silencing complex (RISC).

1.2 miRNA Mechanisms of Action

With few exceptions, metazoan miRNAs base pair with their targets imperfectly and induce translation inhibition. Mature miRNAs, loaded into the RISC, mediate the translational inhibition of target mRNA through several different mechanisms [10]. The RISC blocks the translation initiation at the mRNA-cap-recognition step, by competition with the cytoplasmic cap-binding protein eIF4E (eukaryotic translation initiation factor 4E), which is essential for cap-dependent translation initiation. Furthermore, it has been shown that the RISC component Argonaute 2 (Ago2) binds the anti-association factor eIF6, preventing the assembly of the ribosome. Besides these active inhibitory mechanisms, RISC–miRNA complexes can move the mRNAs they bind to the "P-bodies," specialized cytoplasmic compartments enriched in mRNA-catabolizing enzymes, where translational repression may occur [11]. Since P-bodies contain many enzymes involved in exonucleolytic mRNA degradation, miRNAs could also have a secondary quantitative inhibitory effect on mRNAs.

The identification of miRNA targets is crucial to elucidate the function of miRNAs. The rules that guide miRNA/mRNA interactions are very complex and still under intense investigation [12]. The current paradigm states that a Watson–Crick pairing between the 3'UTR region of the target mRNA and the 5' region of the miRNA centered on nucleotides 2–7, termed "seed sequence," is required for miRNA-mediated inhibition. However, due to the complexity of the miRNA-target interactions, the identification of miRNA targets has proven computationally difficult. Several target prediction algorithms have been developed, but they show a poor overlap between their outputs, suggesting that there are a number of false-negative and most likely also false-positive predictions. To overcome these difficulties, experimental approaches, based on the biochemical purification of the RISC complex and on the identification of the associated mRNAs and miRNAs, have been undertaken [13]. The results revealed that also noncanonical miRNA binding can confer target regulation, confirming that the complexity of miRNA activity is far from being elucidated [14, 15].

1.3   miRNAs as Biomarkers and Therapeutic Targets

The identification of specific miRNAs as key regulators of cell biology has opened new clinical avenues and may allow to develop new diagnostic and/or prognostic tools as much as innovative therapeutic strategies [2, 16, 17]. There is a great potential of exploiting miRNAs for therapeutic purposes, and recent evidence suggests that miRNAs may constitute excellent disease biomarkers. Profiles composed of few hundred miRNAs are more effective in cancer classification than profiles composed of thousands of mRNAs and may be particularly useful when the histopathological analysis is not informative. miRNAs also have a prognostic significance, identifying differential chemotherapy response and survival. Indeed, miRNA-based diagnostic assays have been already developed and approved for certain neoplastic diseases (rosettagenomics.com; asuragen.com). One important criterion for a disease biomarker is the invasive nature of sample procurement. miRNAs have been consistently detected in serum, plasma, and other bodily fluids, and specific miRNA patterns have been associated to pregnancy and to certain diseases [18, 19]. The potential diagnostic/prognostic value of miRNAs in the cardiovascular field has only begun to be investigated, but data obtained so far indicate that their use may not be limited to cancer [2, 20]. Indeed, plasma concentrations of cardiac-specific miR-208 increases in a rat model of isoproterenol-induced myocardial injury, correlating with the concentration of cardiac troponin I, a classic biomarker of myocardial injury [21]. Circulating miR-208 was proposed as biomarker of acute myocardial infarction, as well as miR-1 and miR-499 [20]. Furthermore, it was demonstrated that miR-423-5p, miR-320a, miR-22, and miR-92b are strongly related to the clinical diagnosis of heart failure and correlate with important clinical prognostic parameters [22]. Thus, these miRNAs may represent novel biomarkers of cardiac damage.

As therapeutic targets for cardiovascular diseases, miRNAs could be considered a major breakthrough for at least two reasons: (1) a single miRNA can regulate many target genes and influence a whole gene network, and (2) miRNAs can be efficiently modulated both in vitro and in vivo. miRNAs can be targeted by several tools [2, 17], aiming to reduce the levels of pathogenic or aberrantly expressed miRNAs or to elevate the levels of miRNAs with beneficial functions.

Potential challenges for miRNA therapeutics include the efficiency of the delivery system and its ability to selectively target specific organs and different cell types in the same organ. An example of the relevance of the latter issue is provided by the heart, where fibroblasts or cardiomyocytes targeting can lead to completely different functional outcomes.

The viability of miRNAs as therapeutic targets is confirmed by the fact that a phase 2a clinical trial adopting an anti-miRNA has been completed successfully (NCT01200420). In this case, an LNA-based anti-miRNA targeting a liver-specific miRNA, miR-122, is being developed as a hepatitis C therapy. However, since miR-122 also modulates plasma cholesterol levels [23, 24], it may also have important applications in the cardiovascular arena. This trial showed that the adopted LNA anti-miRNA was safe and well tolerated, with patients displaying only mild adverse events. No dose-limiting toxicities or any discontinuations due to adverse events were reported. Moreover, LNA treatment was associated with dose-dependent, sustained reductions in hepatitis C RNA. Albeit many more clinical studies are needed, this first set of trials indicates that miRNA inhibitors could become an important new class of drugs.

Finally, although the clinical efficacy of miRNA mimics has not yet been demonstrated, this approach represents an attractive means of enhancing miRNA levels for those that are downregulated during disease. For instance, a recent preclinical study demonstrated the efficacy of the systemic delivery of tumor suppressor miRNA mimics in the treatment of lung tumors in mice [25].

2 miRNAs and Ischemic Diseases

Ischemia induces profound changes in miRNA expression [2]. First, we will focus our attention on miRNAs that have been found deregulated upon ischemia in different studies: these may represent "master ischemic" miRNAs, playing a pathogenetic role in one of the different components of tissue response to ischemia, such

Table 1 Overview of ischemia-related miRNAs with relevant validated targets

miRNA	Modulation	Tissue/cell model/disease	Targets	Biological role	References
miR-1	Up	Human CAD/Rat MI	KCNJ2, GJA1	Electrical conductance	Yang et al. [41]
		Rat MI/H9C2 CMC	Igf1	Apoptosis	Shan et al. [40]
		Mouse heart I/R/CMC	Bcl2	Apoptosis	Tang et al. [39]
		Mouse heart IPC		Cardioprotection	Yin et al. [73]
		Rat MI		Ischemic arrhythmogenesis	Lu et al. [71]
	Down	Mouse HLI/C2C12		Myo-differentiation	Greco et al. [53]
		Mouse knock-out	Irx5	Electrical conductance	Zhao et al. [65]
miR-15	Up	Human DCM/ICM/AS			Ikeda et al. [64]
		Mouse MI			van Rooij et al. [47]
		Mouse I/R			Roy et al. [45]
		Mouse MI/Pig MI			Hullinger et al. [32]
miR-21	Up	Mouse heart I/R		Cardioprotection	Yin et al. [68]
		Mouse MI			van Rooij et al. [47]
		Mouse heart IPC			Yin et al. [73]
		Mouse heart I/R/CF	Pten		Roy et al. [45]
miR-24	Up	Mouse heart IPC		Cardioprotection	Yin et al. [73]
miR-29	Down	Mouse MI	Col1a1, Col1a2, Col3a1, Fbn1, Eln	Fibrosis	van Rooij et al. [47]
		Mouse HLI		Fibrosis	Greco et al. [53]
miR-31	Down	Ischemic mouse retina	Pdgf-β, Hif1-α, Fzd4	Anti-angiogenic	Shen et al. [58]
miR-34c	Up	Mouse HLI		Muscle regeneration	Greco et al. [53]
	Up	Mouse HLI		Muscle regeneration	Greco et al. [53]
miR-92a	Up	Mouse HLI/ECs	Itga5, Sirt1, S1pr1, Map2k4	Neovascularization	Bonauer et al. [48]
miR-124	Up	Rat MCAO	Vsnl1	Regeneration	Jeyaseelan et al. [66]
miR-126	Up	Mouse HLI		Neovascularization	van Solingen et al. [49]
miR-135a	Down	Mouse HLI/C2C12		Myo-differentiation	Greco et al. [53]
miR-145	Up	Rat MCAO	Sod2	Antioxidant defense	Dharap et al. [55]

miRNA	Regulation	Tissue/model	Target	Function	Reference
miR-150	Down	Ischemic mouse retina	Pdgf-β, Vefga	Anti-neovascularization	Shen et al. [58]
miR-199a	Down	Mouse MI/pig heart IPC	HIF1-α, SIRT1	Hypoxia	Rane et al. [72]
miR-206	Up	Human CAD/Rat MI	KCNJ2, GJA1	Electrical conductance	Yang et al. [41]
	Down (2d) - Up (14d)	Mouse HLI		Muscle regeneration	Greco et al. [53]
miR-208	Up	Mouse DCM		Electrical conductance	Callis et al. [70]
miR-210	Up	Rat MCAO			Jeyaseelan et al. [66]
		Mouse HLI			Pulkkinen et al. [67]
		Human MI			Bosjancic et al. [69]
		Mouse ischemic wound	E2F3	Antiproliferative	Biswas et al. [74]
miR-214	Up	Human DCM/ICM/AS			Ikeda et al. [64]
		Mouse MI			van Rooij et al. [47]
miR-222	Up	Human DCM/ICM/AS			Ikeda et al. [64]
miR-223	Up	Mouse HLI		Inflammation	Greco et al. [53]
		Mouse MI			van Rooij et al. [47]
		Mouse liver I/R		Hepatic injury	Yu et al. [57]
		Mouse HLI		Inflammation	Greco et al. [53]
miR-290	Up	Rat MCAO	Vsnl1	Regeneration	Jeyaseelan et al. [66]
miR-320	Down	Mouse heart I/R	Hsp20	Cardioprotection	Ren et al. [42]
miR-335	Up	Mouse HLI/C2C12		Muscle regeneration, Myo-differentiation	Greco et al. [53]
miR-499	Down	Rat MI	CnAα, CnA-β	Anti-apoptotic	Wang et al. [75]

AS aortic stenosis, *CAD* coronary artery disease, *CF* cardiac fibroblasts, *CMC* cardiomyocytes, *DCM* dilated cardiomyopathy, *ECs* endothelial cells, *HLI* hind-limb ischemia, *I/R* ischemia/reperfusion, *ICM* ischemic cardiomyopathy, *IPC* ischemic preconditioning, *MCAO* middle cerebral aortic occlusion, *MI* myocardial infarction as hypoxia and angiogenesis (see [26–30] for extensive reviews). Then, two reports in which miRNAs have been targeted to improve cardiac function in preclinical models of myocardial infarction will be described in detail [31, 32], indicating a paradigm of potential of therapeutic strategies based on miRNA targeting.

Table 1 contains an overview of ischemia-related miRNAs with relevant target genes and the relative references.

2.1 Acute Myocardial Infarction

Myocardial ischemic injury results from severe impairment of the coronary blood supply usually produced by thrombosis or other acute alterations of coronary atherosclerotic plaques. The onset of irreversible injury begins after about 20–30 min, and most myocardial infarcts are usually completed within about 3–4 h of onset of severe ischemia. With loss of oxygen, mitochondrial oxidative phosphorylation rapidly stops, with a resulting loss of the major source of ATP production for energy metabolism. Established myocardial infarcts have distinct central and peripheral zones, and the severity of the injury reflects the gradient of perfusion deficit from the center to the periphery of the ischemic zone [33]. miRNAs regulate different aspects of myocardial infarction (MI) that will be discussed in the following sections [2, 34–37].

Cell Survival Muscle-specific miR-1 has been shown to elicit pro-apoptotic responses in cardiomyocytes as well in other cellular systems [38]. In keeping with these results, miR-1 was found upregulated in response to ischemia/reperfusion (I/R) injury in rat heart and in a rat model of MI [39–41]. Indeed, miR-1 is involved in apoptotic cell death induced by cardiac ischemia through the posttranscriptional repression of the anti-apoptotic proteins Bcl2 and IGF-1 [40, 41]. Conversely, miR-320 expression is significantly decreased in the heart following I/R, both in vivo and ex vivo [42]. Transgenic mice with cardiac-specific overexpression of miR-320 revealed an increased extent of apoptosis and infarction size relative to the wild-type controls, whereas anti-miR-320 treatment leads to a reduction of infarction size. The pro-apoptotic role of miR-320 is mediated by the direct inhibition of Hsp20, a known cardioprotective protein previously found upregulated following MI [43]. Among the miRNAs involved in the regulation of cell survival, miR-21 has been shown to play a protective function on cell apoptosis induced after MI in rat hearts [44]. In the early phase of acute MI, miR-21 is significantly downregulated in infarcted areas, whereas its expression is increased in the border zone. The protective effect of miR-21 against ischemia-induced cardiomyocyte death is mediated, at least in part, by the pro-apoptotic targets programmed cell death 4 (PDCD4) and activator protein 1 (AP-1), and it is confirmed in vivo by decreased cell apoptosis in infarcted hearts after miR-21 overexpression [44].

Arrhythmia Arrhythmias are electrical alterations that result in irregular heart beating with consequent insufficient blood pumping. Arrhythmias are often lethal and constitute a major cause for cardiac death in MI. As pointed out in the previous section, miR-1 is upregulated following acute MI [40, 41]. The blockade of miR-1 relieves MI-associated arrhythmias. Indeed, miR-1 overexpression slowed cardiac conduction and depolarized the cytoplasmic membrane, constituting a likely arrhythmogenic cellular mechanism of miR-1. In keeping with an arrhythmogenic role of miR-1 deregulation, connexin 43 (GJA1) and the potassium channel subunit Kir2.1 (KCNJ2) are direct miR-1 targets.

Fibrosis and Remodeling miR-21 was markedly induced and specifically localized in the infarct region of the I/R heart [45]. PTEN is a miR-21 target and following myocardial I/R, miR-21 induction in cardiac fibroblasts inhibits PTEN and leads to an increase of matrix metalloprotease-2, contributing to the cardiac remodeling. In keeping with these findings, miR-21 levels are also selectively increased in fibroblasts of the failing heart, upregulating ERK–MAP kinase activity through inhibition of sprouty homologue 1 [46]. This mechanism regulates fibroblast survival and growth factor secretion, in turn controlling the interstitial fibrosis and cardiac hypertrophy. The expression of miR-29b was found preferentially downregulated in cardiac fibroblasts in the border zone after the occlusion of the left coronary artery [47]. miR-29 family targets multiple mRNAs that encode proteins involved in fibrosis, which is consistent with the experimental correlation between miR-29 downregulation and upregulation of multiple collagens and fibrillin in the infarcted region.

Neo-angiogenesis miR-92a is an endogenous repressor of the angiogenic program in endothelial cells [48]. Moreover, miR-92a inhibition enhances the functional recovery of ischemic tissue both in a mouse model of hind-limb ischemia and following MI. Indeed, miR-92a inhibition improved LV systolic and diastolic function in infarcted hearts, reduced the infarct size, suppressed the number of apoptotic cells, and significantly augmented the number of vessels, particularly in the infarct border zone [48]. In keeping with its pivotal role in angiogenesis [30], miR-126 null mice show reduced survival and defective cardiac and hind-limb neovascularization following ischemia, suggesting a critical function of miR-126 in postischemic neo-angiogenesis [30, 49].

2.2   Other Ischemic Diseases

MiRNAs seem to play an important role in peripheral ischemia. After injury, skeletal muscle undergoes a distinct set of healing phases, consisting of necrosis/degeneration and inflammation in the first few days, regeneration/repair from 2–4 weeks, and fibrosis/scar-tissue formation at 2 or 3 weeks post-injury [50, 51]. Damage, as much as the ensuing regeneration, involves both the vascular and the muscular compartments. After ischemia, a potent neo-angiogenic response is activated, including both capillary sprouting and endothelial progenitor cells recruitment. Myofiber regeneration involves mainly a population of specialized progenitors named satellite cells. Stimulated by several growth factors, these cells become activated, proliferate, and differentiate into multinucleated myotubes and eventually into regenerated myofibers [52]. A subset of miRNAs modulated in a mouse model of hind-limb ischemia was identified [53]. Based on the cell types that express them and on their time of induction after ischemia, these miRNAs can be divided in three classes: degeneration (miR-1, miR-29, miR-135), regeneration (miR-31, miR-34c, miR-206, miR-335, miR-449 and miR-494), and inflammatory (miR 222 and miR-223). Intriguingly, these miRNAs were also modulated in Duchenne muscle dystrophy, a disease characterized by intense skeletal muscle necrosis, regeneration, and enhanced arteriogenesis [54].

Brain transient focal ischemia induces extensive and sustained changes in rat cerebral microRNA expression [55]. Specifically, in situ hybridization displays increased miR-145 levels in the ischemic core. One relevant target of miR-145 is superoxide dismutase-2 (Sod2), a crucial component of the antioxidant defense mechanisms that might promote cell survival after ischemia. Indeed, miR-145 blockade was associated with increased Sod2 levels and smaller cortical infarcts [55].

Hepatic I/R injury is a common problem which occurs in major liver resection and transplantation, which subsequently causes significant parenchymal hepatocyte injury and organ dysfunction [56]. It was recently demonstrated that miR-223 correlates with the severity of hepatic injury, showing the same modulation of ALT and AST, serum markers of injury [57].

Finally, certain miRNAs regulate neo-angiogenesis associated to retinal ischemia. In a mouse model of ischemic retina, miR-31, miR-150, and miR-184 are down-modulated [58]. Intraocular injection of pre-miR-31, pre-miR-150, or pre-miR-184 significantly reduced retinal neovascularization in mice with ischemic retinopathy, suggesting that the deregulation in these miRNAs may contribute, along with transcriptional regulation mechanisms, to the disease phenotype.

2.3   miR-210 Treatment Can Rescue Cardiac Function After Myocardial Infarction

miR-210 can be considered a master miRNA of the hypoxic response [27]. It has been found upregulated by hypoxia in almost all the cells and tissues tested to date; it is upregulated upon brain transient focal ischemia in rats, after human myocardial infarction, and was proposed as a blood biomarker in acute cerebral ischemia. miR-210 is the most induced miRNA in endothelial cells (EC) exposed to hypoxia [59, 60]. miR-210 activity increases EC tubulogenesis and migration, whereas miR-210 blockade in the presence of hypoxia inhibits these processes and induces apoptosis. These effects are mediated, at least in part, by the direct inhibition of the receptor tyrosine kinase ligand Ephrin-A3. Other miR-210 targets have been identified, indicating the miR-210 role in cell cycle regulation, differentiation, mitochondrial metabolism repression, DNA repair, and apoptosis [27, 61]. Since miR-210 pro-angiogenic and anti-apoptotic activities play an integral role in endothelial cell adaptation to hypoxia, it was hypothesized that miR-210 treatment could improve cardiac function after MI through upregulation of angiogenesis and inhibition of cellular apoptosis in the heart [31]. First, miR-210 was transduced in cardiomyocytes cultured in vitro, demonstrating that miR-210 induced the release of several angiogenic factors. Moreover, miR-210-overexpressing cardiomyocytes showed low levels of apoptosis following hypoxia when compared to control cells. Then, to examine whether miR-210 delivery could improve cardiac function after MI, nonviral minicircles were used to carry a miR-210 expression cassette. As novel nonviral vectors, minicircles lack both an origin of replication and the antibiotic selection marker, carrying only short bacterial sequences. Their smaller size confers greater transfection efficiency and the lack of bacterial backbone creates less immunogenicity and longer transgene expression [62]. Using minicircles vectors, miR-210 expression was stable for at least 8 weeks in the animal heart.

To examine whether miR-210 improved cardiac function, adult FVB mice underwent ligation of the mid-left anterior descending (LAD) artery and were injected intramyocardially with miR-210 or a scramble sequence as control. Echocardiography was performed before as well as 2, 4, and 8 weeks after LAD ligation. The miR-210 group displayed significantly higher left ventricular fractional shortening at week 4. Left ventricular end-diastolic volume and end-systolic volume in the miR-210 group were significantly lower than control group, suggesting a more favorable left ventricular remodeling process after miR-210 treatment. At 8 weeks, echocardiography showed a significant improvement of left ventricular fractional shortening upon miR-210 treatment. Histological analysis confirmed decreased cellular apoptosis and increased neovascularization in the miR-210 group after MI. In conclusion, the authors found that miR-210 can improve heart function by upregulating angiogenesis and inhibiting apoptosis. This approach shows that miR-210 delivery through nonviral minicircle may work as a novel therapeutic avenue for treatment of ischemic heart disease.

2.4 Inhibition of miR-15 Protects Against Cardiac Ischemic Injury

The miR-15 family consists of multiple miRNAs (miR-15a, miR-15b, miR-16-1, miR-16-2, miR-195, and miR-497) and is consistently upregulated in different heart diseases [63]. These miRNAs are predicted to influence cardiomyocyte survival by regulating the expression of several pro-survival proteins. Thus, Hullinger et al. hypothesized that elevated levels of miR-15 family members in response to ischemic injury might contribute to a decrease in viable cardiomyocytes. Specifically, they asked if the pharmacological inhibition of miR-15 family can protect against cardiac ischemic injury [32]. To this aim, they used LNA chemically modified,

single-stranded oligonucleotides (LNA anti-miR) that have been shown to effectively inactivate specific miRNAs in vivo through complementary base pairing
[2]. In particular, the LNA-anti-miR used exhibited complementarity to the seed
region that is common to the whole miR-15 family. Thus, the systemic delivery of
this LNA-anti-miR repressed all miR-15 family members, in both murine and
porcine cardiac tissues. Reassuringly, the injected animals showed no evidence of
LNA-associated toxicity or histopathologic abnormalities in the heart, liver, or
kidneys. Then, the functional relevance of miR-15 family inhibition during
ischemia–reperfusion injury was tested. MI was induced in mice by 75 min of
left coronary artery occlusion, followed by reperfusion for either 24 h or 2 weeks;
LNA-anti-miR-15, or controls, were injected intravenously at the onset of reperfusion. As expected, hemodynamic analysis showed a significant increase in LV
end-diastolic pressure in the control group after 24 h of reperfusion. This increase
was prevented by LNA-anti-miR-15 treatment, and miR-15-inhibited mice
displayed a significant decrease of the infarct size. Microarray analysis of infracted
hearts indicated an overrepresentation of negative regulators of cell death in the
LNA-anti-miR-15-treated group. Functional analysis by echocardiography 2 weeks
after induction of the ischemic injury indicated that LNA-anti-miR-15 treatment
resulted in a significant improvement of the ejection fraction, paralleled by a
decrease of cardiac fibrosis.

Taken together, these data demonstrated that the LNA-anti-miR-15 treatment is
able to reduce infarct size, to inhibit cardiac remodeling, and to enhance cardiac
function in response to ischemic damage. These events are likely to be, at least in
part, due to a derepression of anti-apoptotic genes in response to miR-15 inhibition.

3 Conclusions

The reports illustrated were chosen as paradigm to represent the ongoing efforts
toward the optimization of miRNA-based therapies, aimed to the identification of
therapeutic target for the manipulation of cardiac remodeling and function
following MI.

We are just starting to understand the role of miRNAs in gene expression
regulation and the molecular mechanisms underpinning their functions.
Investigating miRNAs expression and function will increase our understanding of
the molecular mechanisms activated by acute ischemia and regulating the
subsequent degenerative and regenerative processes.

Acknowledgments We appreciate the permission of Elsevier Inc. to reprint excerpts from the
publication "microRNA: emerging therapeutic targets in acute ischemic diseases" of Fasanaro P.,
Greco S., Ivan M., Capogrossi M.C., Martelli F. published on Pharmacology & Therapeutics
(2010) January V.125, N.1: 92–104. FM and PF are supported by Ministero della Salute and
Associazione Italiana per la Ricerca sul Cancro (AIRC).

References

1. Bartel, D.P.: MicroRNAs: genomics, biogenesis, mechanism, and function. Cell **116**, 281–297 (2004)
2. Fasanaro, P., Greco, S., Ivan, M., Capogrossi, M.C., Martelli, F.: MicroRNA: emerging therapeutic targets in acute ischemic diseases. Pharmacol. Ther. **125**, 92–104 (2010)
3. Huntzinger, E., Izaurralde, E.: Gene silencing by microRNAs: contributions of translational repression and mRNA decay. Nat. Rev. Genet. **12**, 99–110 (2011)
4. van Rooij, E.: The art of microRNA research. Circ. Res. **108**, 219–234 (2011)
5. Vasudevan, S.: Posttranscriptional upregulation by microRNAs. Wiley interdiscip. Rev. RNA **3**(3), 311–330 (2011)
6. Friedman, R.C., Farh, K.K., Burge, C.B., Bartel, D.P.: Most mammalian mRNAs are conserved targets of microRNAs. Genome Res. **19**, 92–105 (2009)
7. Krol, J., Loedige, I., Filipowicz, W.: The widespread regulation of microRNA biogenesis, function and decay. Nat. Rev. Genet. **11**, 597–610 (2010)
8. Winter, J., Jung, S., Keller, S., Gregory, R.I., Diederichs, S.: Many roads to maturity: microRNA biogenesis pathways and their regulation. Nat. Cell Biol. **11**, 228–234 (2009)
9. Morlando, M., Ballarino, M., Gromak, N., Pagano, F., Bozzoni, I., Proudfoot, N.J.: Primary microRNA transcripts are processed co-transcriptionally. Nat. Struct. Mol. Biol. **15**, 902–909 (2008)
10. Filipowicz, W., Bhattacharyya, S.N., Sonenberg, N.: Mechanisms of post-transcriptional regulation by microRNAs: are the answers in sight? Nat. Rev. Genet. **9**, 102–114 (2008)
11. Parker, R., Sheth, U.: P bodies and the control of mRNA translation and degradation. Mol. Cell **25**, 635–646 (2007)
12. Bartel, D.P.: MicroRNAs: target recognition and regulatory functions. Cell **136**, 215–233 (2009)
13. Thomson, D.W., Bracken, C.P., Goodall, G.J.: Experimental strategies for microRNA target identification. Nucleic Acids Res. **39**, 6845–6853 (2011)
14. Elefant, N., Altuvia, Y., Margalit, H.: A wide repertoire of miRNA binding sites: prediction and functional implications. Bioinformatics **27**, 3093–3101 (2011)
15. Fasanaro, P., Romani, S., Voellenkle, C., Maimone, B., Capogrossi, M.C., Martelli, F.: ROD1 is a seedless target gene of hypoxia-induced mir-210. PLoS One **7**, e44651 (2012)
16. Condorelli, G., Latronico, M.V., Dorn 2nd, G.W.: MicroRNAs in heart disease: putative novel therapeutic targets? Eur. Heart J. **31**, 649–658 (2010)
17. van Rooij, E., Marshall, W.S., Olson, E.N.: Toward microRNA-based therapeutics for heart disease: the sense in antisense. Circ. Res. **103**, 919–928 (2008)
18. Zampetaki, A., Willeit, P., Drozdov, I., Kiechl, S., Mayr, M.: Profiling of circulating microRNAs: from single biomarkers to re-wired networks. Cardiovasc. Res. **93**, 555–562 (2012)
19. Di Stefano, V., Zaccagnini, G., Capogrossi, M.C., Martelli, F.: MicroRNAs as peripheral blood biomarkers of cardiovascular disease. Vascul. Pharmacol. **55**, 111–118 (2011)
20. D'Alessandra, Y., Devanna, P., Limana, F., Straino, S., Di Carlo, A., Brambilla, P.G., Rubino, M., Carena, M.C., Spazzafumo, L., De Simone, M., Micheli, B., Biglioli, P., Achilli, F., Martelli, F., Maggiolini, S., Marenzi, G., Pompilio, G., Capogrossi, M.C.: Circulating microRNAs are new and sensitive biomarkers of myocardial infarction. Eur. Heart J. **31**, 2765–2773 (2010)
21. Ji, X., Takahashi, R., Hiura, Y., Hirokawa, G., Fukushima, Y., Iwai, N.: Plasma miR-208 as a biomarker of myocardial injury. Clin. Chem. **55**, 1944–1949 (2009)
22. Goren, Y., Kushnir, M., Zafrir, B., Tabak, S., Lewis, B.S., Amir, O.: Serum levels of microRNAs in patients with heart failure. Eur. J. Heart Fail. **14**, 147–154 (2012)
23. Krutzfeldt, J., Rajewsky, N., Braich, R., Rajeev, K.G., Tuschl, T., Manoharan, M., Stoffel, M.: Silencing of microRNAs in vivo with 'antagomirs'. Nature **438**, 685–689 (2005)

24. Esau, C., Davis, S., Murray, S.F., Yu, X.X., Pandey, S.K., Pear, M., Watts, L., Booten, S.L., Graham, M., McKay, R., Subramaniam, A., Propp, S., Lollo, B.A., Freier, S., Bennett, C.F., Bhanot, S., Monia, B.P.: miR-122 regulation of lipid metabolism revealed by in vivo antisense targeting. Cell Metab. **3**, 87–98 (2006)
25. Trang, P., Wiggins, J.F., Daige, C.L., Cho, C., Omotola, M., Brown, D., Weidhaas, J.B., Bader, A.G., Slack, F.J.: Systemic delivery of tumor suppressor microRNA mimics using a neutral lipid emulsion inhibits lung tumors in mice. Mol. Ther. **19**, 1116–1122 (2011)
26. Ivan, M., Harris, A.L., Martelli, F., Kulshreshtha, R.: Hypoxia response and microRNAs: no longer two separate worlds. J. Cell. Mol. Med. **12**, 1426–1431 (2008)
27. Devlin, C., Greco, S., Martelli, F., Ivan, M.: miR-210: more than a silent player in hypoxia. IUBMB Life **63**, 94–100 (2011)
28. Gorospe, M., Tominaga, K., Wu, X., Fahling, M., Ivan, M.: Post-transcriptional control of the hypoxic response by RNA-binding proteins and microRNAs. Front. Mol. Neurosci. **4**, 7 (2011)
29. Suarez, Y., Sessa, W.C.: MicroRNAs as novel regulators of angiogenesis. Circ. Res. **104**, 442–454 (2009)
30. Wang, S., Olson, E.N.: AngiomiRs–key regulators of angiogenesis. Curr. Opin. Genet. Dev. **19**, 205–211 (2009)
31. Hu, S., Huang, M., Li, Z., Jia, F., Ghosh, Z., Lijkwan, M.A., Fasanaro, P., Sun, N., Wang, X., Martelli, F., Robbins, R.C., Wu, J.C.: MicroRNA-210 as a novel therapy for treatment of ischemic heart disease. Circulation **122**, S124–S131 (2010)
32. Hullinger, T.G., Montgomery, R.L., Seto, A.G., Dickinson, B.A., Semus, H.M., Lynch, J.M., Dalby, C.M., Robinson, K., Stack, C., Latimer, P.A., Hare, J.M., Olson, E.N., van Rooij, E.: Inhibition of miR-15 protects against cardiac ischemic injury. Circ. Res. **110**, 71–81 (2012)
33. Buja, L.M.: Myocardial ischemia and reperfusion injury. Cardiovasc. Pathol. **14**, 170–175 (2005)
34. Ye, Y., Perez-Polo, J.R., Qian, J., Birnbaum, Y.: The role of microRNA in modulating myocardial ischemia–reperfusion injury. Physiol. Genomics **43**, 534–542 (2011)
35. Frost, R.J., van Rooij, E.: miRNAs as therapeutic targets in ischemic heart disease. J. Cardiovasc. Transl. Res. **3**, 280–289 (2010)
36. Dorn 2nd, G.W.: MicroRNAs in cardiac disease. Transl. Res. **157**, 226–235 (2011)
37. Heyn, J., Hinske, C., Mohnle, P., Luchting, B., Beiras-Fernandez, A., Kreth, S.: MicroRNAs as potential therapeutic agents in the treatment of myocardial infarction. Curr. Vasc. Pharmacol. **9**, 733–740 (2011)
38. Xu, C., Lu, Y., Pan, Z., Chu, W., Luo, X., Lin, H., Xiao, J., Shan, H., Wang, Z., Yang, B.: The muscle-specific microRNAs miR-1 and miR-133 produce opposing effects on apoptosis by targeting HSP60, HSP70 and caspase-9 in cardiomyocytes. J. Cell Sci. **120**, 3045–3052 (2007)
39. Tang, Y., Zheng, J., Sun, Y., Wu, Z., Liu, Z., Huang, G.: MicroRNA-1 regulates cardiomyocyte apoptosis by targeting Bcl-2. Int. Heart J. **50**, 377–387 (2009)
40. Shan, Z.X., Lin, Q.X., Fu, Y.H., Deng, C.Y., Zhou, Z.L., Zhu, J.N., Liu, X.Y., Zhang, Y.Y., Li, Y., Lin, S.G., Yu, X.Y.: Upregulated expression of miR-1/miR-206 in a rat model of myocardial infarction. Biochem. Biophys. Res. Commun. **381**, 597–601 (2009)
41. Yang, B., Lin, H., Xiao, J., Lu, Y., Luo, X., Li, B., Zhang, Y., Xu, C., Bai, Y., Wang, H., Chen, G., Wang, Z.: The muscle-specific microRNA miR-1 regulates cardiac arrhythmogenic potential by targeting GJA1 and KCNJ2. Nat. Med. **13**, 486–491 (2007)
42. Ren, X.P., Wu, J., Wang, X., Sartor, M.A., Qian, J., Jones, K., Nicolaou, P., Pritchard, T.J., Fan, G.C.: MicroRNA-320 is involved in the regulation of cardiac ischemia/reperfusion injury by targeting heat-shock protein 20. Circulation **119**, 2357–2366 (2009)
43. De Celle, T., Vanrobaeys, F., Lijnen, P., Blankesteijn, W.M., Heeneman, S., Van Beeumen, J., Devreese, B., Smits, J.F., Janssen, B.J.: Alterations in mouse cardiac proteome after in vivo myocardial infarction: permanent ischaemia versus ischaemia–reperfusion. Exp. Physiol. **90**, 593–606 (2005)

44. Dong, S., Cheng, Y., Yang, J., Li, J., Liu, X., Wang, X., Wang, D., Krall, T.J., Delphin, E.S., Zhang, C.: MicroRNA expression signature and the role of microRNA-21 in the early phase of acute myocardial infarction. J. Biol. Chem. **284**(43), 29514–29525 (2009)

45. Roy, S., Khanna, S., Hussain, S.R., Biswas, S., Azad, A., Rink, C., Gnyawali, S., Shilo, S., Nuovo, G.J., Sen, C.K.: MicroRNA expression in response to murine myocardial infarction: miR-21 regulates fibroblast metalloprotease-2 via phosphatase and tensin homologue. Cardiovasc. Res. **82**, 21–29 (2009)

46. Thum, T., Gross, C., Fiedler, J., Fischer, T., Kissler, S., Bussen, M., Galuppo, P., Just, S., Rottbauer, W., Frantz, S., Castoldi, M., Soutschek, J., Koteliansky, V., Rosenwald, A., Basson, M.A., Licht, J.D., Pena, J.T., Rouhanifard, S.H., Muckenthaler, M.U., Tuschl, T., Martin, G.R., Bauersachs, J., Engelhardt, S.: MicroRNA-21 contributes to myocardial disease by stimulating MAP kinase signalling in fibroblasts. Nature **456**, 980–984 (2008)

47. van Rooij, E., Sutherland, L.B., Thatcher, J.E., DiMaio, J.M., Naseem, R.H., Marshall, W.S., Hill, J.A., Olson, E.N.: Dysregulation of microRNAs after myocardial infarction reveals a role of miR-29 in cardiac fibrosis. Proc. Natl. Acad. Sci. USA **105**, 13027–13032 (2008)

48. Bonauer, A., Carmona, G., Iwasaki, M., Mione, M., Koyanagi, M., Fischer, A., Burchfield, J., Fox, H., Doebele, C., Ohtani, K., Chavakis, E., Potente, M., Tjwa, M., Urbich, C., Zeiher, A.M., Dimmeler, S.: MicroRNA-92a controls angiogenesis and functional recovery of ischemic tissues in mice. Science **324**, 1710–1713 (2009)

49. van Solingen, C., Seghers, L., Bijkerk, R., Duijs, J.M., Roeten, M.K., van Oeveren-Rietdijk, A.M., Baelde, H.J., Monge, M., Vos, J.B., de Boer, H.C., Quax, P.H., Rabelink, T.J., van Zonneveld, A.J.: Antagomir-mediated silencing of endothelial cell specific microRNA-126 impairs ischemia-induced angiogenesis. J. Cell. Mol. Med. **13**(8A), 1577–1585 (2008)

50. Huard, J., Li, Y., Fu, F.H.: Muscle injuries and repair: current trends in research. J. Bone Joint Surg. Am. **84-A**, 822–832 (2002)

51. Blaisdell, F.W.: The pathophysiology of skeletal muscle ischemia and the reperfusion syndrome: a review. Cardiovasc. Surg. **10**, 620–630 (2002)

52. Hawke, T.J., Garry, D.J.: Myogenic satellite cells: physiology to molecular biology. J. Appl. Physiol. **91**, 534–551 (2001)

53. Greco, S., De Simone, M., Colussi, C., Zaccagnini, G., Fasanaro, P., Pescatori, M., Cardani, R., Perbellini, R., Isaia, E., Sale, P., Meola, G., Capogrossi, M.C., Gaetano, C., Martelli, F.: Common micro-RNA signature in skeletal muscle damage and regeneration induced by Duchenne muscular dystrophy and acute ischemia. FASEB J. **23**(10), 3335–3346 (2009)

54. Straino, S., Germani, A., Di Carlo, A., Porcelli, D., De Mori, R., Mangoni, A., Napolitano, M., Martelli, F., Biglioli, P., Capogrossi, M.C.: Enhanced arteriogenesis and wound repair in dystrophin-deficient mdx mice. Circulation **110**, 3341–3348 (2004)

55. Dharap, A., Bowen, K., Place, R., Li, L.C., Vemuganti, R.: Transient focal ischemia induces extensive temporal changes in rat cerebral microRNAome. J. Cereb. Blood Flow Metab. **29**, 675–687 (2009)

56. Serracino-Inglott, F., Habib, N.A., Mathie, R.T.: Hepatic ischemia–reperfusion injury. Am. J. Surg. **181**, 160–166 (2001)

57. Yu, C.H., Xu, C.F., Li, Y.M.: Association of microRNA-223 expression with hepatic ischemia/reperfusion injury in mice. Dig. Dis. Sci. **54**(11), 2362–2366 (2008)

58. Shen, J., Yang, X., Xie, B., Chen, Y., Swaim, M., Hackett, S.F., Campochiaro, P.A.: MicroRNAs regulate ocular neovascularization. Mol. Ther. **16**, 1208–1216 (2008)

59. Voellenkle, C., van Rooij, J., Guffanti, A., Brini, E., Fasanaro, P., Isaia, E., Croft, L., David, M., Capogrossi, M.C., Moles, A., Felsani, A., Martelli, F.: Deep-sequencing of endothelial cells exposed to hypoxia reveals the complexity of known and novel microRNAs. RNA **18**, 472–484 (2012)

60. Fasanaro, P., D'Alessandra, Y., Di Stefano, V., Melchionna, R., Romani, S., Pompilio, G., Capogrossi, M.C., Martelli, F.: MicroRNA-210 modulates endothelial cell response to hypoxia and inhibits the receptor tyrosine kinase ligand Ephrin-A3. J. Biol. Chem. **283**, 15878–15883 (2008)

61. Fasanaro, P., Greco, S., Lorenzi, M., Pescatori, M., Brioschi, M., Kulshreshtha, R., Banfi, C., Stubbs, A., Calin, G.A., Ivan, M., Capogrossi, M.C., Martelli, F.: An integrated approach for experimental target identification of hypoxia-induced miR-210. J. Biol. Chem. **284**, 35134–35143 (2009)

62. Huang, M., Chen, Z., Hu, S., Jia, F., Li, Z., Hoyt, G., Robbins, R.C., Kay, M.A., Wu, J.C.: Novel minicircle vector for gene therapy in murine myocardial infarction. Circulation **120**, S230–S237 (2009)

63. Small, E.M., Frost, R.J., Olson, E.N.: MicroRNAs add a new dimension to cardiovascular disease. Circulation **121**, 1022–1032 (2010)

64. Ikeda, S., Kong, S.W., Lu, J., Bisping, E., Zhang, H., Allen, P.D., Golub, T.R., Pieske, B., Pu, W.T.: Altered microRNA expression in human heart disease. Physiol. Genomics **31**, 367–373 (2007)

65. Zhao, Y., Ransom, J.F., Li, A., Vedantham, V., von Drehle, M., Muth, A.N., Tsuchihashi, T., McManus, M.T., Schwartz, R.J., Srivastava, D.: Dysregulation of cardiogenesis, cardiac conduction, and cell cycle in mice lacking miRNA-1-2. Cell **129**, 303–317 (2007)

66. Jeyaseelan, K., Lim, K.Y., Armugam, A.: MicroRNA expression in the blood and brain of rats subjected to transient focal ischemia by middle cerebral artery occlusion. Stroke **39**, 959–966 (2008)

67. Pulkkinen, K., Malm, T., Turunen, M., Koistinaho, J., Yla-Herttuala, S.: Hypoxia induces microRNA miR-210 in vitro and in vivo ephrin-A3 and neuronal pentraxin 1 are potentially regulated by miR-210. FEBS Lett. **582**, 2397–2401 (2008)

68. Yin, C., Wang, X., Kukreja, R.C.: Endogenous microRNAs induced by heat-shock reduce myocardial infarction following ischemia-reperfusion in mice. FEBS Lett. **582**, 4137–4142 (2008)

69. Bostjancic, E., Zidar, N., Glavac, D.: MicroRNA microarray expression profiling in human myocardial infarction. Dis. Markers **27**, 255–268 (2009)

70. Callis, T.E., Pandya, K., Seok, H.Y., Tang, R.H., Tatsuguchi, M., Huang, Z.P., Chen, J.F., Deng, Z., Gunn, B., Shumate, J., Willis, M.S., Selzman, C.H., Wang, D.Z.: MicroRNA-208a is a regulator of cardiac hypertrophy and conduction in mice. J. Clin. Invest. **119**, 2772–2786 (2009)

71. Lu, Y., Zhang, Y., Shan, H., Pan, Z., Li, X., Li, B., Xu, C., Zhang, B., Zhang, F., Dong, D., Song, W., Qiao, G., Yang, B.: MicroRNA-1 downregulation by propranolol in a rat model of myocardial infarction: a new mechanism for ischaemic cardioprotection. Cardiovasc. Res. **84**, 434–441 (2009)

72. Rane, S., He, M., Sayed, D., Vashistha, H., Malhotra, A., Sadoshima, J., Vatner, D.E., Vatner, S.F., Abdellatif, M.: Downregulation of miR-199a derepresses hypoxia-inducible factor-1alpha and Sirtuin 1 and recapitulates hypoxia preconditioning in cardiac myocytes. Circ. Res. **104**, 879–886 (2009)

73. Yin, C., Salloum, F.N., Kukreja, R.C.: A novel role of microRNA in late preconditioning: upregulation of endothelial nitric oxide synthase and heat shock protein 70. Circ. Res. **104**, 572–575 (2009)

74. Biswas, S., Roy, S., Banerjee, J., Hussain, S.R., Khanna, S., Meenakshisundaram, G., Kuppusamy, P., Friedman, A., Sen, C.K.: Hypoxia inducible microRNA 210 attenuates keratinocyte proliferation and impairs closure in a murine model of ischemic wounds. Proc. Natl. Acad. Sci. USA **107**, 6976–6981 (2011)

75. Wang, J.X., Jiao, J.Q., Li, Q., Long, B., Wang, K., Liu, J.P., Li, Y.R., Li, P.F.: miR-499 regulates mitochondrial dynamics by targeting calcineurin and dynamin-related protein-1. Nat. Med. **17**(71–78) (2011)

The Role of Cardiac Magnetic Resonance in Selecting Patients with Left Ventricular Dysfunction Undergoing Surgical Ventricular Reconstruction

Serenella Castelvecchio and Lorenzo Menicanti

Abstract Surgical ventricular reconstruction (SVR) has gained wide acceptance over the past 10 years as a surgical treatment for ischemic heart failure. However, data from the largest randomized trial have questioned the real additional benefit of SVR in respect of coronary artery bypass grafting (CABG) alone, outlining the need to improve patient selection. To this aim, we investigated the role of cardiac magnetic resonance (CMR) in characterizing the extent of myocardial fibrosis and its prognostic value in patients affected by ischemic cardiomyopathy (ICM).

Twenty-five patients (mean age 68 ± 8 years) affected by ICM, a left ventricle ejection fraction (EF) < 40 %, and referred for CABG underwent *late gadolinium enhancement* (LGE)-CMR before and 6 months after surgery and were included in Group 1. Forty patients (mean age 65 ± 10 years) affected by ICM, a left ventricle EF < 40 %, and referred for CABG plus SVR underwent the same protocol and were included in Group 2. In Group 1, patients showed a high percentage of viable myocardium, a percentage of recoverable myocardium higher than 50 %, and a low percentage of hyperenhanced tissue, indicating a low degree of fibrosis. At 6 months, end-diastolic volume index (EDVI) decreased by 23 %, end-systolic volume index (ESVI) decreased by 38 %, and ejection fraction (EF) increased by 13 absolute points. Conversely, in Group 2, a lower percentage of viable tissue and a higher percentage of hyperenhanced tissue identified patients with more dilated ventricles and lower EF. At the multivariate analysis, only the percentage of scar

S. Castelvecchio (✉)
Division of Cardiac Surgery, IRCCS Policlinico San Donato, San Donato Milanese, Milan, Italy
e-mail: castelvecchio.serenella@gmail.com

L. Menicanti
Division of Cardiac Surgery, IRCCS Policlinico San Donato, San Donato Milanese, Milan, Italy
e-mail: menicanti@libero.it

N. Grieco et al. (eds.), *New Diagnostic, Therapeutic and Organizational Strategies for Acute Coronary Syndromes Patients*, Contributions to Statistics,
DOI 10.1007/978-88-470-5379-3_8, © Springer-Verlag Italia 2013

tissue at the basal portion has been resulted to be significantly associated with an adverse outcome ($P = 0.04$, OR 1.26, 95 % CI 1.01–1.58) in Group 2.

In patients affected by ICM and LV dysfunction, the myocardial tissue characterization by LGE–CMR might be useful in predicting the postoperative adverse outcome after SVR.

1 Introduction

Despite many breakthroughs in cardiovascular medicine, myocardial infarction (MI) and heart failure (HF) are still among the most major public health challenges in the developed countries. HF is associated with ischemic heart disease ("ischemic cardiomyopathy" [ICM]) in a percentage of patients ranging from 46 to 68 % [1]. Research has been very effective in delivering major advances in therapy of ischemic HF patients, including drugs, device therapy, and surgery. However, despite advances in different therapeutic strategies, the prognosis for patients with chronic ischemic HF remains poor and determining the best management is challenging.

Surgical ventricular reconstruction (SVR) combined with coronary artery bypass grafting (CABG) has gained wide acceptance over the past 10 years as an optional therapeutic strategy aimed to reduce LV volumes through the exclusion of the scar tissue (Fig. 1), thereby restoring the physiological volume and shape and improving LV function and clinical status [2, 3]. However, the most recent released results from the STICH trial have called into question the additional benefit either of CABG over medical therapy or of CABG plus LVR in patients affected by ischemic heart failure and LV dysfunction, suggesting the need to improve patient selection [4]. To this aim, it is reasonable to hypothesize that noninvasive assessment of myocardium in patients with ICM can guide treatment.

Cardiac magnetic resonance (CMR) is increasingly being used for the noninvasive imaging of the HF population, and it is nowadays the gold standard imaging technique to assess myocardial anatomy, regional and global function, and the extension of the scar [5]. A basic CMR protocol includes the assessment of LV volumes and global and regional function based on contiguous short-axis cine images. The greatest usefulness of CMR is in the detection of myocardial scar with *late gadolinium enhancement* (LGE). LGE imaging visualizes irreversible damage (myocardial scar or fibrosis) due to an accumulation of contrast agent in areas with increased extracellular space. In LGE images, viable myocardium appears dark, whereas necrotic or fibrotic myocardial tissue appears bright (Fig. 2). LGE has unprecedented spatial resolution and can determine the transmural extent of scar, which is not possible with other imaging modalities. At the same time, CMR offers the opportunity to assess thickness and function of the remaining nonenhanced viable myocardial tissue ("the remote regions"), which may be hibernating (ischemic but viable myocardium likely for functional recovering after CABG) or nonischemic but dysfunctional because of the high

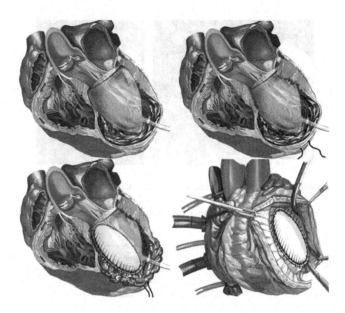

Fig. 1 The LVR procedure (schematic). *Upper panel*: The mannequin is inside the ventricle (on the *left*); the *circular* suture follows the curvature of the mannequin to reshape the ventricle in elliptical way (on the *right*). *Lower panel*: The patch is used to close the ventricular opening

local tension that reduces shortening and likely for functional improvement after volume reduction obtained through LVR, as previously demonstrated. Commercially available software dedicated to LV analysis now provides a semiautomated assessment of thickening, global and regional function, and the percentage and extension of scarred tissue, which can potentially be combined in predicting myocardial viability without a need for pharmacologic stress ("integrated approach").

In this study, we sought to investigate the role of LGE–CMR in characterizing the extent of myocardial fibrosis and its prognostic value in patients affected by ischemic cardiomyopathy (ICM).

2 Population and Methods

For inclusion in the study, patients were required to have the following (a) a previous myocardial infarction (MI), either Q or non-Q; (b) coronary artery disease confirmed by a coronary angiography; (c) congestive heart failure symptoms; and (d) LV ejection fraction (EF) < 40 % preoperatively.

Patients who had acute MI within 3 months and LVEF > 40 % at the baseline echocardiography were excluded from the study. Further exclusion criteria included standard contraindications to CMR imaging. Baseline echocardiography

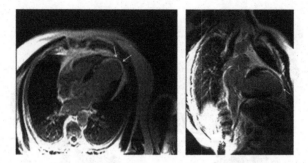

Fig. 2 Contrast-enhanced cardiac MR imaging. Images have been acquired in a patient after a large myocardial infarction in the left anterior descending artery territory. After gadolinium administration, late gadolinium enhancement indicates a scar in the anterior wall and in the apex

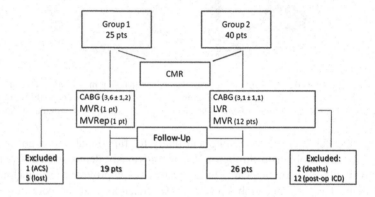

Fig. 3 *MVR* mitral valve repair, *MVRep* mitral valve replacement, *ACS* acute coronary syndrome

was firstly performed in all patients for assessment of left ventricular function and wall motion. The choice of adding SVR to CABG alone was performed according to the presence of anterior akinesia or dyskinesia of the left ventricle amenable to surgical ventricular reconstruction. Therefore, the study population was divided in two groups according to the surgical treatment. Twenty-five patients (23 males, aged 68 ± 8 years) affected by ICM and selected for CABG underwent CMR before and 6 months after surgery and were included in Group 1. Forty patients (38 males, aged 65 ± 10 years) affected by ICM and selected for CABG plus LVR underwent the same protocol and were included in Group 2 (Fig. 3).

2.1 CMR Protocol and Image Analysis

We used a 1.5-T unit with 40-mT/m gradient power (Magnetom Sonata, Siemens, Erlangen, Germany) and a four-channel cardiothoracic coil. The same protocol was used before and after surgery. Electrocardiographically triggered short-axis, four chamber, and long-axis images were obtained with a true fast imaging with steady-state free precession (FISP) sequence acquired with the following technical parameters: TR/TE = 4.5/1.5 ms, temporal resolution 47 ms, FA = 80°, thickness 7 mm, and pixel size from 3.5 to 3.9 mm^2. Each patient was intravenously administered with 0.1 mmol/kg of gadobenate dimeglumine (Gd-BOPTA, MultiHance®, Bracco Imaging SpA, Milano, Italy) at a rate of 2–3 ml/s, followed by 20 ml of saline solution at the same rate using an automated power injector (Spectris, Medrad, Indianola, PA, USA). After 10 min from contrast material injection, inversion-recovery-prepared turbo gradient-echo (fast low-angle shot) multi-slice short-axis, four chamber, and long-axis sequences were acquired with the following technical parameters: TR/TE = 4/1.37 ms, temporal resolution 700 ms, FA = 10°, thickness 5 mm, and pixel size from 4.5 to 5.1 mm^2. The inversion time was individually optimized between 220 and 280 ms. Optimization of the inversion time was assessed by scout images captured at various time points and choosing those which provided the best nulling effect. The images were subsequently analyzed using an integrating imaging system (*COMPASS*, Chase Medical, Richardson, TX). Cine images were segmented semiautomatically by a reader with 3 years of experience in CMR to obtain ejection fraction (EF), end-diastolic volume (EDV) normalized to body surface area (EDV index, EDVI), and end-systolic volume index (ESVI) of the LV before and after SVR. The same observer analyzed the LGE spatial distribution globally and regionally (according to the 17-segment model to standardize LV segmentation) at the basal, mid, and apical LV, with the aim to examine its distribution between the two groups and the impact on postoperative outcome (Figs. 4 and 5).

3 Results

In Group 1, patients showed a high percentage of viable myocardium, a percentage of recoverable myocardium higher than 50 %, and a low percentage of hyperenhanced tissue, indicating a low degree of fibrosis (percentage of scarred tissue) (Fig. 6, left panel). At 6 months, end-diastolic volume index (EDVI) decreased by 23 %, end-systolic volume index (ESVI) decreased by 38 %, and ejection fraction (EF) increased by 13 absolute points (hemodynamic results are reported in Table 1). In Group 2, a lower percentage of viable tissue and a higher percentage of hyperenhanced tissue (Fig. 6, right panel) identified patients with more dilated ventricles and lower EF (Table 2 for comparison).

At follow-up, adverse events (AE) included two deaths for worsening of HF, three hospitalizations for recurrence of HF, and one hospitalization for ventricular tachycardia. At univariate analysis, preoperative EDVI, ESVI, and the percentage of scar tissue at the basal portion of LV were predictors of poor outcome (defined as the occurrence of the abovementioned AE) (Table 3). At the multivariate analysis, only the percentage of scar tissue at the basal portion has been resulted to be significantly predictor of adverse outcome ($P = 0.04$, OR 1.26, 95 % CI 1.01–1.58).

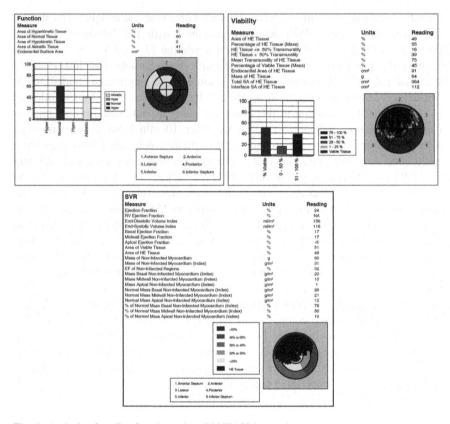

Fig. 4 Analysis of cardiac function using *COMPASS* integrating system

4 Discussion

This study shows that the detection and the extent of myocardial fibrosis as evaluated by LGE–CMR might provide additional information including the following (a) firstly, a higher likelihood for functional recovery after CABG alone in presence of a high percentage of viable myocardium and a low percentage of hyperenhanced tissue and (b) the relevance of assessing the "remote regions" where the detection of the scar may predict an adverse clinical outcome.

The prognostic value of myocardial viability was assessed in a series of retrospective and prospective nonrandomized which showed that the presence of viable myocardium recognized with several noninvasive imaging techniques such as ultrasound, nuclear perfusion techniques, and resonance magnetic correlates with prognosis. Two meta-analysis, including a total of 5,305 patients with postischemic left ventricular dysfunction undergoing dobutamine test or nuclear techniques, confirmed the strong association between myocardial viability and improvement

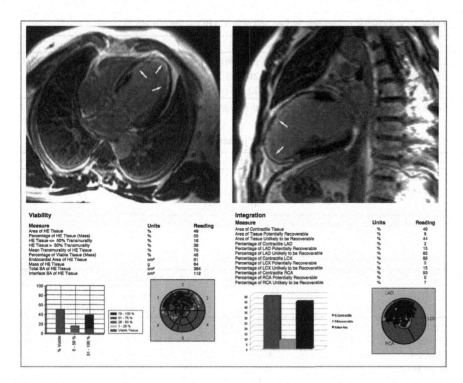

Fig. 5 Analysis of cardiac function using *COMPASS* integrating system

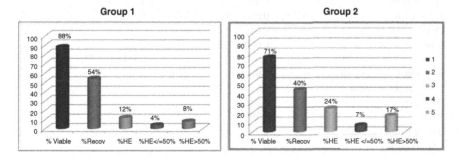

Fig. 6 Viability parameters as observed in Group 1 (CABG only) and Group 2 (CABG plus SVR). % Viable: percentage of viable tissue (mass); % recov: area of tissue potentially recoverable; %HE: percentage of hyperenhanced tissue (mmass); %HE $\leq$ 50 %: hyperenhanced tissue with a percentage of transmurality $\leq$ 50 %; %HE $>$ 50 %: hyperenhanced tissue with a percentage of transmurality $>$ 50 %

of survival after revascularization, while the absence of myocardial viability was neutral, regardless of treatment either medical or surgical [6, 7]. However, the more recent results from the STICH hypothesis 1 subgroup analysis showed that the

Table 1 Volumetric parameters before and after CABG alone (Group 1)

	Preop	Post-op change
EDVI (ml/m^2)	114 ± 24 (106)	88 ± 26 (72) − 23 %
ESVI (ml/m^2)	88 ± 26 (72)	51 ± 7 (41) − 38 %
EF (%)	29 ± 13 (25)	42 ± 14 (41) + 13

EDVI end-diastolic volume index, *ESVI* end-systolic volume index, *EF* ejection fraction

Table 2 Comparison in baseline volumetric parameters between Groups 1 and 2

	Group 1	Group 2
EDVI (ml/m^2)	114 ± 24 (106)	155 ± 35 (135)
ESVI (ml/m^2)	88 ± 26 (72)	118 ± 48 (108)
EF (%)	29 ± 13 (25)	23 ± 9 (21)

EDVI end-diastolic volume index; *ESVI* end-systolic volume index; *EF* ejection fraction

Table 3 Preoperative risk factors for adverse events

	Univariate	Multivariate
	P value	*P* value OR (95 % confidence interval)
Age	0.17	
Gender, male	0.69	
Diabetes	0.97	
Hypertension	0.13	
Hyperlipidemia	0.59	
NHYA class	0.13	
EDVI (ml/m^2)	0.04	0.16
ESVI (ml/m^2)	0.03	0.09
EF (%)	0.91	
% of scar mass basal	0.009	0.04 1.26 (1.01–1.58)
% of scar mass midwall	0.06	
% of scar mass apical	0.62	
IM grade	0.88	
E/A	0.80	
DT (ms)	0.79	
PAPs (mmHg)	0.54	

assessment of myocardial viability, using single-photon emission computed tomography (SPECT), dobutamine echocardiography, or both did not allow to identify patients with different benefits in terms of survival after CABG, as compared to medical therapy alone [8]. Beside the fact that different techniques give different information making the results difficult to be compared, CMR was not performed in the STICH trial in both revascularization and reconstruction hypothesis patients. Furthermore, while there are data in the literature supporting the basal portion of the

LV as an important component of the systolic function, no data are available coming from CMR integrating imaging system of patients undergoing SVR. Therefore, we believe that these results might be useful (a) to systematically follow up patients after the first MI in order to better characterize the postischemic LV remodeling and (b) to select those patients who could benefit from SVR at the best for the presence of a scar to be excluded *not* involving the basal portion of LV.

Unfortunately, the exclusion of patients with pacemakers or devices for cardiac resynchronization therapy and the potential reduction of image quality in patients with significant arrhythmia or severe shortness of breath limit the use of CMR.

5 Conclusions

Although further studies, including a larger population, should be performed, preoperative assessment of myocardial status on LGE–CMR might be useful to predict functional recovery and adverse outcome after different surgical options, and, most important, to select the best surgical therapy, from which the greatest benefit can be expected.

References

1. Gheorghiade, M., Sopko, G., De Luca, L., et al.: Navigating the crossroads of coronary artery disease and heart failure. Circulation **114**, 1202–1213 (2006)
2. Menicanti, L., Castelvecchio, S.: Left ventricular reconstruction concomitant to coronary artery bypass grafting: when and how? Curr. Opin. Cardiol. **26**, 523–527 (2011)
3. Menicanti, L., Castelvecchio, S., Ranucci, M., et al.: Surgical therapy for ischemic heart failure: single-center experience with surgical anterior ventricular restoration. J. Thorac. Cardiovasc. Surg. **134**, 433–441 (2007)
4. Jones, R.H., Velazquez, E.J., Michler, R.E., STICH Hypothesis 2 Investigators, et al.: Coronary bypass surgery with or without surgical ventricular reconstruction. N. Engl. J. Med. **360**, 1705–1717 (2009)
5. Schuster, A., Morton, G., Chiribiri, A.: Imaging in the management of ischemic cardiomyopathy. J. Am. Coll. Cardiol. **59**, 359–370 (2012)
6. Allman, K.C., Shaw, L.J., Hachamovitch, R., Udelson, J.E.: Myocardial viability testing and impact of revascularization on prognosis in patients with coronary artery disease and left ventricular dysfunction: a meta-analysis. J. Am. Coll. Cardiol. **39**, 1151–1158 (2002)
7. Bourque, J.M., Hasselblad, V., Velazquez, E.J., et al.: Revascularization in patients with coronary artery disease, left ventricular dysfunction, and viability: a meta-analysis. Am. Heart J. **146**, 621–627 (2003)
8. Bonow, R.O., Maurer, G., Lee, K.L., STICH Trial Investigators, et al.: Myocardial viability and survival in ischemic left ventricular dysfunction. N. Engl. J. Med. **364**, 1617–25 (2011)

Chronic Kidney Disease in Acute Myocardial Infarction: Clinical Relevance and Novel Potential Fields of Investigation

Giancarlo Marenzi, Marina Camera, Cristina Banfi, Gualtiero Colombo, Marta Brambilla, Maura Brioschi, and Elena Tremoli

Abstract In patients with acute coronary syndromes (ACS), chronic kidney disease (CKD) is highly prevalent and associated with poor short- and long-term outcomes. Management of patients with CKD presenting with ACS is more complex than in the general population because of the lack of well-designed randomized trials assessing therapeutic strategies in such patients. The almost uniform exclusion of patients with CKD from randomized studies evaluating new targeted therapies for ACS, coupled with concerns about further deterioration of renal function and therapy-related toxic effects, may explain the less frequent use of proven medical therapies in this subgroup of high-risk patients. In this chapter, we summarize the current evidence regarding the epidemiology and the clinical and prognostic relevance of CKD in ACS patients, in particular with respect to unresolved issues and uncertainties regarding recommended medical therapies and coronary revascularization strategies. Moreover, we suggest some novel promising fields of investigation in order to identify adjunctive therapeutic targets and pharmacological therapies that may favorably affect their otherwise poor prognosis.

G. Marenzi (✉) • C. Banfi • G. Colombo • M. Brambilla • M. Brioschi
Centro Cardiologico Monzino, IRCCS, Milan, Italy
e-mail: giancarlo.marenzi@cardiologicomonzino.it; cristina.banfi@cardiologicomonzino.it;
gualtiero.colombo@cardiologicomonzino.it; marta.brambillla@cardiologicomonzino.it;
maura.brioschi@cardiologicomonzino.it

M. Camera • E. Tremoli
Department of Pharmacological Sciences, Università degli Studi di Milano, Centro
Cardiologico Monzino, IRCCS, Milan, Italy
e-mail: marina.camera@cardiologicomonzino.it; elena.tremoli@cardiologicomonzino.it

N. Grieco et al. (eds.), *New Diagnostic, Therapeutic and Organizational Strategies for
Acute Coronary Syndromes Patients*, Contributions to Statistics,
DOI 10.1007/978-88-470-5379-3_9, © Springer-Verlag Italia 2013

1 Introduction

Chronic kidney disease (CKD) is associated with accelerated atherogenesis, due to the presence of both traditional and nontraditional (related to the underlying uremic state) risk factors, and any degree of renal insufficiency portends a worsened prognosis in patients with coronary artery disease [1, 2]. The adverse influence of CKD has been also demonstrated in the setting of acute coronary syndromes (ACS) [3–11]. Indeed, among ACS patients, CKD doubles mortality rates and is third only to cardiogenic shock and congestive heart failure as a predictor of mortality [12]. Antithrombotic agents and percutaneous coronary interventions (PCI) are clearly emerging as the cornerstones of treatment patterns in patients presenting with ACS [13]. Despite the increasing number of CKD patients with a broad range of ACS at presentation, evidence-based data with established or newer drugs and interventional strategies are still lacking in this population because CKD patients have typically been excluded from randomized trials. Ideally, these are the patients to whom recent therapeutic advances should be aggressively applied, in order to minimize their increased risk. However, application of strategies for reducing cardiovascular morbidity and mortality seem to be limited in CKD patients, when compared to patients with normal renal function.

Chronic kidney disease is present in a substantial proportion of patients with ACS; indeed, large registries report that almost 40 % of patients with non-ST-elevation myocardial infarction (NSTEMI) and 30 % of those with ST-elevation myocardial infarction (STEMI) have CKD, as defined by an estimated glomerular filtration rate <60 ml/min/1.73 m^2 [14, 15].

The currently high prevalence of CKD patients in the setting of ACS represents a strong incentive to development of targeted strategies from well-designed research, which will ultimately reduce the burden of risk in this population and achieve improved outcomes. Recognition of the mechanisms associated with increased risk of ACS patients with CKD is a critical challenge to better determine where to concentrate the efforts in future trials and to validate novel and effective therapies for these high-risk patients.

2 Prognostic Relevance of CKD in Acute Coronary Syndromes

In ACS, CKD represents a potent and independent risk factor for adverse outcome. Although the mechanisms underlying the poor prognosis of this vulnerable population are not fully understood, it is conceivable that the interplay between extensive comorbidities, more severe disease on presentation with ACS, underutilization of known cardio-protective therapies, less aggressive treatment, more frequent errors in dosing with excess toxicity from conventional therapies, and unique pathobiology of CKD has a considerable role.

The fundamental work of Herzog et al. [3] was the initial observation that revealed the poor prognosis faced by patients with end-stage renal disease (ESRD) who suffer from acute myocardial infarction. Using the US Renal Data System database, the investigators examined the outcome of 34,189 patients on long-term dialysis after a first episode of acute myocardial infarction and documented an in-hospital mortality of 26 % and 1-year and 2-year mortality rates of 59 % and 73 %, respectively. These observations were confirmed by Chertow et al. [4] who reported a 30-day mortality rate of 20 % and a 1-year mortality rate of 53 % after acute myocardial infarction in 640 patients with ESRD. Beattie et al. [5] extended the investigation to patients with advanced renal dysfunction who were not on dialysis therapy. They analyzed a prospective coronary care unit registry of 1,724 patients with STEMI admitted over an 8-year period at a single tertiary care center. Patients were stratified into groups based on different creatinine clearance (CrCl) values. A graded rise in in-hospital complications and death rate, as well as a reduction in long-term survival, were observed across increasing renal dysfunction strata. This study, as well as another one by McCullough et al. [16], showed a similar graded increase in the relative risk of atrial and ventricular arrhythmias, heart block, asystole, pulmonary congestion, and cardiogenic shock in parallel with progressive renal impairment. Two following large studies revealed the significant morbidity and mortality risk faced by STEMI patients with even minor renal insufficiency [6, 7]. All these, as well as further studies, like a Danish study evaluating 6,252 patients included in the TRACE (TRAndolapril Cardiac Evaluation) register [17], and a recent large study, the ACTION (Acute Coronary Treatment and Intervention Outcomes Network) registry, including 19,029 STEMI patients [14], support the evidence of a strikingly high mortality in STEMI patients with CKD.

Finally, in the VALIANT (Valsartan in Acute Myocardial Infarction Trial) study, the outcome of CKD patients remained worse also after hospital discharge, at a long-term (3 years) follow-up, despite an apparent optimal post-discharge treatment (all patients received valsartan, captopril, or a combination of both) [18]. These results suggest that even appropriate post-discharge therapy, given in a timely manner, may not be sufficient to improve post-acute myocardial infarction outcome in CKD population.

Several observational studies have found that also in the setting of NSTEMI in-hospital outcomes and mid- to long-term mortality are worse among patients with CKD [8, 9, 11, 19] (Fig. 1). The GRACE (Global Registry of Acute Coronary Events) study, a large prospective multinational registry, including the full spectrum of patients with ACS, evaluated the prognostic impact of serum creatinine (sCr) levels on in-hospital mortality and adverse outcomes in 11,774 NSTEMI patients [8]. Patients were divided into three groups according to their estimated CrCl values: >60 ml/min or normal renal function (including patients with minimally impaired renal function), 30–60 ml/min or moderate renal insufficiency, and <30 ml/min or severe renal insufficiency. In comparison with patients with normal renal function, patients with moderate and severe renal insufficiency were at a significantly increased risk of hospital mortality and major bleeding episodes

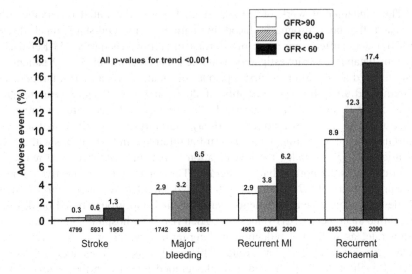

Fig. 1 Incidence of adverse events in patients with non-ST segment elevation myocardial infarction/unstable angina (NSTEMI/UA) by glomerular filtration rate (GFR) groups: stroke, in-hospital TIMI major bleeding, recurrent myocardial infarction (MI), and recurrent ischemia at 30 days. The number of patients within each subgroup is displayed at the bottom of each bar. GFR is expressed in ml/min/1.73 m^2 [11]

(Fig. 1). Other studies have definitely confirmed the close association between CKD and increased risk of death in patients with NSTE-ACS at presentation [10, 12, 20].

3   Treatment of Patients with ACS and CKD

Treatment of ACS in patients with CKD is particularly problematic. Traditionally, patients with advanced CKD and ESRD receiving dialysis have not been included in randomized ACS trials evaluating either medical or interventional therapies. Thus, only scarce data deriving from limited observational studies are available, and to date, no optimal treatment strategy has been defined for this subgroup of patients. Doubts still exist on how CKD patients should be treated in the early phase of STEMI and NSTEMI. In particular, there are concerns about the use of aggressive reperfusion strategy (fibrinolytic therapy and primary PCI). Undoubtedly, landmark megatrials have shown the benefit of thrombolytic agents and primary PCI in reducing mortality in patients with STEMI. However, in most of these trials, no subgroup analysis was performed in patients with CKD, and scarce data have been published on the use of coronary reperfusion strategies in these patients. So, despite the evidence of a clear benefit deriving from pharmacologic and mechanical coronary reperfusion in STEMI, the best strategy for STEMI patients with CKD remains elusive.

As early coronary angiography and revascularization has been shown to be a more effective strategy for high-risk patients with NSTE-ACS [13], a major issue in CKD patients is the question as to whether renal insufficiency or the coronary revascularization procedure (PCI or coronary bypass surgery) may be the cause of their worsened hospital outcome. In most of the studies focusing on the prognostic role of renal insufficiency, patients were more likely to be treated conservatively with anti-ischemic and antithrombotic agents, while PCI was performed only in patients with recurrent myocardial ischemia. Furthermore, in the studies in which the advantage of an early invasive strategy was demonstrated [21–23], patients with advanced CKD, as well as those with an increased risk of bleeding, were excluded. With these limitations, a retrospective study examined the interaction between CrCl, outcomes, and the use of an early invasive strategy in 2,190 patients with NSTE-ACS enrolled in the TACTICS-TIMI 18 (Treat Angina with Aggrastat and Determine Cost of Therapy with an Invasive or Conservative Strategy) trial [19]. Irrespective of treatment strategy, mild to moderate decrease in renal function was a potent risk factor for adverse outcome, with a concomitant increase in endpoints such as death, acute myocardial infarction, and rehospitalization at 30 and 180 days. Routine invasive management, however, was associated with a statistically significant reduction in the same end points, across most categories of CKD, at the predictable price of a significant increase in major and minor bleeding.

Two recent large studies, the ACTION registry [14] and the SWEDEHEART (Swedish Web-System for Enhancement and Development of Evidence-Based Care in Heart Disease Evaluated According to Recommended Therapies) study [24], including 30,462 and 23,262 NSTEMI patients, respectively, confirmed the close association between CKD severity and increased in-hospital and 1-year mortality rates. In particular, the SWEDEHEART study demonstrated a gradient of progressively lower advantage from PCI vs. medical therapy with no advantage, in terms of 1-year mortality, going from patients with normal renal function to patients with increasing CKD severity, with no benefit at all for those with severe (Stage IV) CKD [24]. The lack of overall benefit in this subset of patients is possibly explained by a higher incidence of PCI-associated complications that may overweight the advantage deriving from coronary revascularization. Indeed, most post-PCI complications associated with poor short-term and long-term outcomes, such as contrast-induced nephropathy [25], coronary stent thrombosis and restenosis [26, 27], underlying coronary artery disease progression [1], and bleedings [8] (Fig. 2), have been found to occur more frequently in CKD than in no CKD patients.

Refinement of the antithrombotic strategies among CKD patients in ACS setting is still a major and unmet need. The challenge is daunting because, on the one hand, CKD is associated with prolongation of bleeding time and abnormal platelet aggregation and adhesion, and on the other hand, a state of hypercoagulation has been demonstrated with high levels of von Willebrand factor; fibrinogen; factors VII, VIII, and XII; and enhanced thrombin generation [28]. The combination of these alterations puts the patient with CKD at risk, simultaneously, for thrombosis and hemorrhage. Thus, use of well-established antiplatelet drugs, such as aspirin

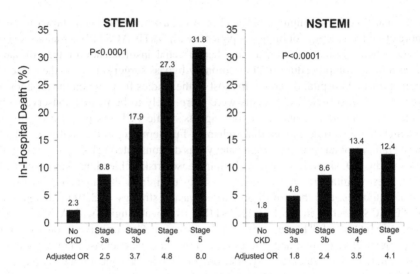

Fig. 2 Crude rates and adjusted odds ratios (OR) for in-hospital death by chronic kidney disease (CKD) stages among patients presenting with STEMI and NSTEMI [14]

and clopidogrel, should be weighed against bleeding risk in renal patients. Finally, impaired renal clearance of many pharmacological agents may increase the probability of overdosing in patients with reduced renal function, further increasing their bleeding risk [29].

4 Identification of Mechanisms Underlying the Increased Risk of ACS Patients with CKD

As previously stated, increasing evidence indicates that individuals with CKD are more likely to die of cardiovascular disease than to develop kidney failure and that renal insufficiency represents the most important independent predictor of adverse prognosis in most cardiovascular events, including ACS. The mechanisms linking CKD to increased mortality risk in patients with ACS have not been completely defined but are possibly associated with the presence of an abnormal pathologic background, including platelets activation and coagulation processes, inflammatory response, and cellular characteristics and functions. Indeed, renal insufficiency associated to coronary artery disease often causes modifications in platelet function and reactivity, influencing signal transduction pathways, which ultimately lead to the thrombotic complications associated with the disease [30]. A better understanding of the pathophysiology of platelet activation that occurs in CKD patients is therefore mandatory in order to improve targeted interventions.

More recently, the development of technologies for whole genome sequencing, proteomics, transcriptomics, and metabolomics will extend the analysis to a more complete range of potential susceptibility variants and will support more explicit modeling of the joint effects of genes and environment. The availability of these technologies does not diminish the importance of rigorous phenotyping and appropriate study designs in all the endeavors to understand the etiopathogenesis of coronary artery disease but through the collaborative efforts at both bench and bedside will have the potential to expand our understanding and translate discoveries into clinically useful applications that will have a major impact on public health.

4.1 Platelet Function Revisited

As far as the involvement of platelets is concerned, they play a pivotal role in the pathogenesis and in the thrombotic complications of ACS and are nowadays recognized to have also an important role in inflammation, being the source of inflammatory mediators [31]. Activated platelets not only release preformed proteins, but studies in the past few years have highlighted their biosynthetic potential [32, 33].

Indeed, taking advantage of the technological progress and of the new methodologies available, recent studies have completely changed our knowledge of the functions and activities exerted by platelet not only in the intravascular compartment but also in the extravascular milieu [34].

For a long time, platelets have been considered biological simple cells, with a limited repertoire of responses, merely in charge of primary hemostasis. Recent findings, however, indicate that they perform novel and complex activities, and many of them are still to be discovered. Platelets have been considered not able to express new gene products because they lack a nucleus; we know today that platelets indeed retain an average of 3–7,000 of megakaryocyte-derived messenger RNA (mRNA), which are used by the translational machinery for protein biosynthesis [32]. Instead of being short-acting cells when organized into a clot, as it was originally thought, platelets are long-lived and can mediate cell-cell interaction for many hours after initial activation.

Taking advantage from these new findings in the platelet biology, the contribution of these cells in atherothrombosis has been deeply revised. By one hand, platelets are no more considered key player only in thrombus formation occurring upon plaque rupture but, by releasing a set of inflammatory mediators, they take part since the early phases of development of the disease, when they contribute to endothelial and monocyte activation, and thus to plaque progression [33, 34]. On the other hand, the evidence that activated platelets expose on their membrane functionally active tissue factor (TF), the main cellular activator of blood coagulation cascade, makes the platelets no longer only the assembly site for coagulation enzyme complexes, but themselves become elements capable of activating the coagulation cascade leading to thrombin generation [35]. It is of note, on this regard, that platelets from ACS patient express on their surface higher amount of functionally active TF compared to platelets than stable angina (SA) patients. This results in a higher platelet-associated thrombin generation capacity which, in turn, contributes to the prothrombotic phenotype of ACS patients [36].

Increased expression of platelet-associated TF expression has been reported in other pathological conditions characterized by an increased thrombotic propensity, such as essential thrombocythemia [37], cancer [38], and diabetes [39]. Based on these evidences, in the attempt to shed light on the thrombotic propensity of CKD patients, it will be of interest to investigate TF expression in this clinical setting.

4.2 The Transcriptomic and Proteomic Approach for the Discovery of Novel Biomarkers

We should also consider that the "omic" approaches to the global study of the products of gene expression, including transcriptomics and proteomics, will play a major role in elucidating the functional role of gene products and in understanding their involvement in disease such as CKD (Fig. 3).

Indeed, as previously mentioned, platelets have the capacity of protein synthesis through translation of megakaryocyte-derived mRNAs, which may influence pathophysiological functions. Transcript profiling and proteomics have the potential to transform the way we analyze platelet biology by determining platelet mRNA/protein composition and changes upon stimulation and/or disease [32, 40]. Platelets represent an attractive and relatively simple model for such studies, because they lack nuclear DNA and their genome consists of a small set of megakaryocyte-derived mRNA transcripts: the complete pool of platelet RNAs is significantly smaller than the transcriptome of a nucleated cell.

It has been reported that specific platelet mRNAs may vary in clinical conditions such as systemic lupus erythematosus [41], sickle-cell disease [42], and STEMI [43]. We recently identified a transcript profile that is significantly different in platelet from stable angina (SA) and NSTEMI patients [44]. Bioinformatics analysis identified three altered biological processes that significantly distinguished the type of coronary artery disease: protein complex assembly, signal transduction, and response to stress. In addition, a number of genes involved in cell adhesion were overexpressed in NSTEMI, with respect to SA platelets. All these gene categories are of apparent relevance for platelet reactivity. Despite these progresses, no information is still available on the changes that may occur in ACS patients with CKD. Identification of disease-associated platelet-specific transcripts is of particular relevance in platelet pathophysiology, since it may lead to the discovery of novel therapeutic targets.

The term proteome describes the entire collection of proteins of an organism, the "proteome," which includes products arising from events such as the processing of mRNA transcripts and posttranslational modifications (i.e., glycosylation, phosphorylation, and oxidation) [45]. The distinctive feature of proteomics-based

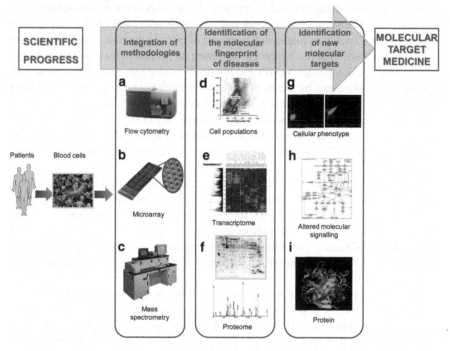

Fig. 3 New methodologies applied to the study of platelet phenotype and functions. The scientific progress has enabled the development of new methodologies that are applied to the study of platelet phenotype and functions in physiology as well as in diseases. Flow cytometry (**a**, **d**, and **g**) is a laser-based, biophysical technology routinely used in the diagnosis of health disorders but has many other applications in basic research and clinical practice allowing the detection of cell-associated biomarkers. A DNA microarray (**b**, **e**, and **h**) is a collection of microscopic DNA spots attached to a solid surface. DNA microarrays are used to measure the expression levels of large numbers of transcripts simultaneously. The transcriptome is the set of all RNA molecules produced in a population of cells. The proteome is the entire set of expressed proteins in a given type of cells or an organism at a given time under defined conditions. Proteomic studies are commonly based on the resolution of protein mixtures by two-dimensional gel electrophoresis and subsequent identification of the resolved proteins by protein sequencing or mass spectrometry (**c**, **f**, and **i**). The application of these molecular methods allows the characterization of the molecular fingerprint of the disease and the identification of new molecular targets as well as of new biomarkers. The information obtained with the use of these methodologies is then correlated with clinical data, such as the stage of disease or the response to pharmacological treatment, with the ultimate goal of helping the physician to tailor the treatment to each patient

studies is that they are focused on the interactions of multiple proteins and their role as part of a biological system rather than the structure and function of one single component. The proteome is, therefore, the result of a dynamic, ongoing process of protein expression and modification and varies both under normal physiological conditions and in response to pathophysiological stresses.

There is an increasing interest in applying the analysis of the plasma proteome to the study of ACS, since plasma is not only the most accessible clinical sample for diagnosis but also it is a protein-rich reservoir of information that contains traces of what has been encountered by the blood during its perfusion throughout the body.

Circulating microparticles (MP) and lipoproteins also represent attractive targets for biomarker discovery by means of proteomics. Both the number and composition of plasma MP are altered in many diseases, including ACS [46].

A promising strategy, to circumvent the complexity of the proteomic analysis of the atherosclerotic plaque due to its intrinsic heterogeneous cellular composition, is to study the cellular behavior of the cells involved in atherosclerosis in the setting of ACS.

Given the central role of macrophages in plaque rupture and thrombosis, their behavior is of great interest in the study of ACS. These cells are in contact with the diseased endovascular lumen and may yield information about the processes occurring in this setting. The monocytes from ACS patients displayed indeed a significantly different expression in proteins involved in energetic and metabolic processes, hydrolysis, blood transport, contraction, inflammation, and neo-angiogenesis [47].

To establish if ACS could induce specific changes in the expression, distribution, or amount of proteins in platelets, due to the key role played in atherogenesis, we performed a proteomic analysis of human platelets from patients with ACS showing, for the first time, that there is a significant difference in the expression of six proteins not previously connected with the disease in comparison with control subjects: two enzymes involved in energy metabolism (LDH and OGDH), three proteins associated with cytoskeleton-based processes (γ-actin, coronin 1B, and pleckstrin), and one involved in protein degradation (PSB8). In particular, we found that the glycolytic enzyme LDH is upregulated, in terms of protein and activity, in patients with NSTEMI in comparison with patients with SA and controls, which suggests more activated energy metabolism in ACS [48].

All these findings open the possibility to explore in future studies if the reported variations of protein expression in monocytes and platelets of ACS patients play a role in the pathophysiology of this disorder. Also, they bring the opportunity to investigate if some of the proteins, whose expression was altered, could be potential candidates for risk assessment in ACS. Nevertheless, prospective studies correlating their plasma levels with ACS patients' outcome are needed to confirm this issue.

In brief, with the application of proteomic techniques, biomarkers can be identified without previous knowledge of their involvement in the pathogenesis of ACS and its comorbidities, such as CKD. However, the field is in the early stages of evolution, and large-scale clinical studies are required to validate the usefulness of newly identified biomarkers in the diagnosis, risk stratification, treatment, and follow-up of cardiovascular diseases.

5 Conclusions

Chronic kidney disease—of any degree—is present in a substantial proportion of patients with ACS and represents a potent and independent risk factor for adverse outcome. Unfortunately, data are still limited regarding the value of most therapeutic interventions, because CKD patients with ACS have typically been excluded from randomized trials. Thus, our current challenge is to further study these high-risk patients in order to identify adjunctive therapeutic targets and pharmacological therapies that may favorably affect their otherwise poor prognosis.

References

1. Sarnak, M.J., Levey, A.S., Schoolwerth, A.C., Coresh, J., Culleton, B., Hamm, L.L., McCullough, P.A., Kasiske, B.L., Kelepouris, E., Klag, M.J., Parfrey, P., Pfeffer, M., Raij, L., Spinosa, D.J., Wilson, P.W.: Kidney disease as a risk factor for development of cardiovascular disease: a statement from the American Heart Association Councils on Kidney in Cardiovascular Disease, High Blood Pressure Research, Clinical Cardiology, and Epidemiology and Prevention. Hypertension 42(5), 1050–1065 (2003). 10.1161/01.HYP.0000102971. 85504.7c42/5/1050 [pii]
2. Go, A.S., Chertow, G.M., Fan, D., McCulloch, C.E., Hsu, C.Y.: Chronic kidney disease and the risks of death, cardiovascular events, and hospitalization. N. Engl. J. Med. 351(13), 1296–1305 (2004). 10.1056/NEJMoa041031351/13/1296 [pii]
3. Herzog, C.A., Ma, J.Z., Collins, A.J.: Poor long-term survival after acute myocardial infarction among patients on long-term dialysis. N. Engl. J. Med. 339(12), 799–805 (1998). 10.1056/NEJM199809173391203
4. Chertow, G.M., Normand, S.L., Silva, L.R., McNeil, B.J.: Survival after acute myocardial infarction in patients with end-stage renal disease: results from the cooperative cardiovascular project. Am. J. Kidney Dis. 35(6), 1044–1051 (2000). S0272-6386(00)70038-2 [pii]
5. Beattie, J.N., Soman, S.S., Sandberg, K.R., Yee, J., Borzak, S., Garg, M., McCullough, P.A.: Determinants of mortality after myocardial infarction in patients with advanced renal dysfunction. Am. J. Kidney Dis. 37(6), 1191–1200 (2001). S0272-6386(01)32229-1 [pii]10.1053/ajkd.2001.24522
6. Wright, R.S., Reeder, G.S., Herzog, C.A., Albright, R.C., Williams, B.A., Dvorak, D.L., Miller, W.L., Murphy, J.G., Kopecky, S.L., Jaffe, A.S.: Acute myocardial infarction and renal dysfunction: a high-risk combination. Ann. Intern. Med. 137(7), 563–570 (2002). 200210010–00007 [pii]
7. Shlipak, M.G., Heidenreich, P.A., Noguchi, H., Chertow, G.M., Browner, W.S., McClellan, M.B.: Association of renal insufficiency with treatment and outcomes after myocardial infarction in elderly patients. Ann. Intern. Med. 137(7), 555–562 (2002). 200210010–00006 [pii]
8. Santopinto, J.J., Fox, K.A., Goldberg, R.J., Budaj, A., Pinero, G., Avezum, A., Gulba, D., Esteban, J., Gore, J.M., Johnson, J., Gurfinkel, E.P.: Creatinine clearance and adverse hospital outcomes in patients with acute coronary syndromes: findings from the global registry of acute coronary events (GRACE). Heart 89(9), 1003–1008 (2003)
9. James, S.K., Lindahl, B., Siegbahn, A., Stridsberg, M., Venge, P., Armstrong, P., Barnathan, E.S., Califf, R., Topol, E.J., Simoons, M.L., Wallentin, L.: N-terminal pro-brain natriuretic peptide and other risk markers for the separate prediction of mortality and subsequent myocardial infarction in patients with unstable coronary artery disease: a global utilization of strategies to open occluded

arteries (GUSTO)-IV substudy. Circulation **108**(3), 275–281 (2003). 10.1161/01.CIR. 0000079170.10579.DC01.CIR.0000079170.10579.DC [pii]

10. Keeley, E.C., Kadakia, R., Soman, S., Borzak, S., McCullough, P.A.: Analysis of long-term survival after revascularization in patients with chronic kidney disease presenting with acute coronary syndromes. Am. J. Cardiol. **92**(5), 509–514 (2003). S0002914903007161 [pii]

11. Gibson, C.M., Karha, J., Giugliano, R.P., Roe, M.T., Murphy, S.A., Harrington, R.A., Green, C.L., Schweiger, M.J., Miklin, J.S., Baran, K.W., Palmeri, S., Braunwald, E., Krucoff, M.W.: Association of the timing of ST-segment resolution with TIMI myocardial perfusion grade in acute myocardial infarction. Am. Heart J. **147**(5), 847–852 (2004). 10.1016/j. ahj.2003.11.015S0002870303008287 [pii]

12. Masoudi, F.A., Plomondon, M.E., Magid, D.J., Sales, A., Rumsfeld, J.S.: Renal insufficiency and mortality from acute coronary syndromes. Am. Heart J. **147**(4), 623–629 (2004). 10.1016/ j.ahj.2003.12.010S0002870303008743 [pii]

13. Bassand, J.P., Hamm, C.W., Ardissino, D., Boersma, E., Budaj, A., Fernandez-Aviles, F., Fox, K.A., Hasdai, D., Ohman, E.M., Wallentin, L., Wijns, W.: Guidelines for the diagnosis and treatment of non-ST-segment elevation acute coronary syndromes. Eur. Heart J. **28**(13), 1598–1660 (2007). ehm161 [pii]10.1093/eurheartj/ehm161

14. Fox, C.S., Muntner, P., Chen, A.Y., Alexander, K.P., Roe, M.T., Cannon, C.P., Saucedo, J.F., Kontos, M.C., Wiviott, S.D.: Use of evidence-based therapies in short-term outcomes of ST-segment elevation myocardial infarction and non-ST-segment elevation myocardial infarction in patients with chronic kidney disease: a report from the National Cardiovascular Data Acute Coronary Treatment and Intervention Outcomes Network registry. Circulation **121**(3), 357–365 (2010). CIRCULATIONAHA.109.865352 [pii]10.1161/ CIRCULATIONAHA.109.865352

15. Wong, J.A., Goodman, S.G., Yan, R.T., Wald, R., Bagnall, A.J., Welsh, R.C., Wong, G.C., Kornder, J., Eagle, K.A., Steg, P.G., Yan, A.T.: Temporal management patterns and outcomes of non-ST elevation acute coronary syndromes in patients with kidney dysfunction. Eur. Heart J. **30**(5), 549–557 (2009). ehp014 [pii]10.1093/eurheartj/ehp014

16. McCullough, P.A., Soman, S.S., Shah, S.S., Smith, S.T., Marks, K.R., Yee, J., Borzak, S.: Risks associated with renal dysfunction in patients in the coronary care unit. J. Am. Coll. Cardiol. **36**(3), 679–684 (2000). S0735-1097(00)00774-9 [pii]

17. Sorensen, C.R., Brendorp, B., Rask-Madsen, C., Kober, L., Kjoller, E., Torp-Pedersen, C.: The prognostic importance of creatinine clearance after acute myocardial infarction. Eur. Heart J. **23**(12), 948–952 (2002). 10.1053/euhj.2001.2989S0195668X01929896 [pii]

18. Anavekar, N.S., McMurray, J.J., Velazquez, E.J., Solomon, S.D., Kober, L., Rouleau, J.L., White, H.D., Nordlander, R., Maggioni, A., Dickstein, K., Zelenkofske, S., Leimberger, J.D., Califf, R.M., Pfeffer, M.A.: Relation between renal dysfunction and cardiovascular outcomes after myocardial infarction. N. Engl. J. Med. **351**(13), 1285–1295 (2004). 10.1056/ NEJMoa041365351/13/1285 [pii]

19. Januzzi, J.L., Cannon, C.P., DiBattiste, P.M., Murphy, S., Weintraub, W., Braunwald, E.: Effects of renal insufficiency on early invasive management in patients with acute coronary syndromes (the TACTICS-TIMI 18 trial). Am. J. Cardiol. **90**(11), 1246–1249 (2002). S0002914902028448 [pii]

20. Wison, S., Foo, K., Cunningham, J., Cooper, J., Deaner, A., Knight, C., Ranjadayalan, K., Timmis, A.D.: Renal function and risk stratification in acute coronary syndromes. Am. J. Cardiol. **91**(9), 1051–1054 (2003). S0002914903001474 [pii]

21. Wallentin, L., Lagerqvist, B., Husted, S., Kontny, F., Stahle, E., Swahn, E.: Outcome at 1 year after an invasive compared with a non-invasive strategy in unstable coronary-artery disease: the FRISC II invasive randomised trial. FRISC II investigators. Fast revascularisation during instability in coronary artery disease. Lancet **356**(9223), 9–16 (2000)

22. Cannon, C.P., Weintraub, W.S., Demopoulos, L.A., Vicari, R., Frey, M.J., Lakkis, N., Neumann, F.J., Robertson, D.H., DeLucca, P.T., DiBattiste, P.M., Gibson, C.M., Braunwald, E.: Comparison of early invasive and conservative strategies in patients with unstable coronary

syndromes treated with the glycoprotein IIb/IIIa inhibitor tirofiban. N. Engl. J. Med. **344**(25), 1879–1887 (2001). 10.1056/NEJM200106213442501
23. Fox, K.A., Poole-Wilson, P.A., Henderson, R.A., Clayton, T.C., Chamberlain, D.A., Shaw, T.R., Wheatley, D.J., Pocock, S.J.: Interventional versus conservative treatment for patients with unstable angina or non-ST-elevation myocardial infarction: the British Heart Foundation RITA 3 randomised trial. Randomized intervention trial of unstable angina. Lancet **360**(9335), 743–751 (2002). S014067360209894X [pii]
24. Szummer, K., Lundman, P., Jacobson, S.H., Schon, S., Lindback, J., Stenestrand, U., Wallentin, L., Jernberg, T.: Influence of renal function on the effects of early revascularization in non-ST-elevation myocardial infarction: data from the Swedish web-system for enhancement and development of evidence-based care in heart disease evaluated according to recommended therapies (SWEDEHEART). Circulation **120**(10), 851–858 (2009). CIRCULATIONAHA.108.838169 [pii]10.1161/CIRCULATIONAHA.108.838169
25. Marenzi, G., Lauri, G., Assanelli, E., Campodonico, J., De Metrio, M., Marana, I., Grazi, M., Veglia, F., Bartorelli, A.L.: Contrast-induced nephropathy in patients undergoing primary angioplasty for acute myocardial infarction. J. Am. Coll. Cardiol. **44**(9), 1780–1785 (2004). S0735-1097(04)01611-0 [pii]
26. Iakovou, I., Schmidt, T., Bonizzoni, E., Ge, L., Sangiorgi, G.M., Stankovic, G., Airoldi, F., Chieffo, A., Montorfano, M., Carlino, M., Michev, I., Corvaja, N., Briguori, C., Gerckens, U., Grube, E., Colombo, A.: Incidence, predictors, and outcome of thrombosis after successful implantation of drug-eluting stents. JAMA **293**(17), 2126–2130 (2005). 293/17/2126 [pii] 10.1001/jama.293.17.2126
27. Sadeghi, H.M., Stone, G.W., Grines, C.L., Mehran, R., Dixon, S.R., Lansky, A.J., Fahy, M., Cox, D.A., Garcia, E., Tcheng, J.E., Griffin, J.J., Stuckey, T.D., Turco, M., Carroll, J.D.: Impact of renal insufficiency in patients undergoing primary angioplasty for acute myocardial infarction. Circulation **108**(22), 2769–2775 (2003). 10.1161/01.CIR.0000103623.63687.2101. CIR.0000103623.63687.21 [pii]
28. Sagripanti, A., Barsotti, G.: Bleeding and thrombosis in chronic uremia. Nephron **75**(2), 125–139 (1997)
29. Alexander, K.P., Chen, A.Y., Roe, M.T., Newby, L.K., Gibson, C.M., Allen-LaPointe, N.M., Pollack, C., Gibler, W.B., Ohman, E.M., Peterson, E.D.: Excess dosing of antiplatelet and antithrombin agents in the treatment of non-ST-segment elevation acute coronary syndromes. JAMA **294**(24), 3108–3116 (2005). 294/24/3108 [pii]10.1001/jama.294.24.3108
30. Boccardo, P., Remuzzi, G., Galbusera, M.: Platelet dysfunction in renal failure. Semin. Thromb. Hemost. **30**(5), 579–589 (2004). 10.1055/s-2004-835678
31. Lievens, D., von Hundelshausen, P.: Platelets in atherosclerosis. Thromb. Haemost. **106**(5), 827–838 (2011). 10.1160/TH11-08-0592
32. Gnatenko, D.V., Dunn, J.J., McCorkle, S.R., Weissmann, D., Perrotta, P.L., Bahou, W.F.: Transcript profiling of human platelets using microarray and serial analysis of gene expression. Blood **101**(6), 2285–2293 (2003). 10.1182/blood-2002-09-2797 2002-09-2797 [pii]
33. Zimmerman, G.A., Weyrich, A.S.: Signal-dependent protein synthesis by activated platelets: new pathways to altered phenotype and function. Arterioscler. Thromb. Vasc. Biol. **28**(3), s17–24 (2008). 28/3/s17 [pii]10.1161/ATVBAHA.107.160218
34. Gawaz, M., Langer, H., May, A.E.: Platelets in inflammation and atherogenesis. J. Clin. Invest. **115**(12), 3378–3384 (2005). 10.1172/JCI27196
35. Camera, M., Frigerio, M., Toschi, V., Brambilla, M., Rossi, F., Cottell, D.C., Maderna, P., Parolari, A., Bonzi, R., De Vincenti, O., Tremoli, E.: Platelet activation induces cell-surface immunoreactive tissue factor expression, which is modulated differently by antiplatelet drugs. Arterioscler. Thromb. Vasc. Biol. **23**(9), 1690–1696 (2003). 10.1161/01. ATV.0000085629.23209.AA 01.ATV.0000085629.23209.AA [pii]
36. Brambilla, M., Camera, M., Colnago, D., Marenzi, G., De Metrio, M., Giesen, P.L., Balduini, A., Veglia, F., Gertow, K., Biglioli, P., Tremoli, E.: Tissue factor in patients with acute coronary syndromes: expression in platelets, leukocytes, and platelet-leukocyte aggregates. Arterioscler.

Thromb. Vasc. Biol. **28**(5), 947–953 (2008). ATVBAHA.107.161471 [pii]10.1161/ATVBAHA. 107.161471

37. Falanga, A., Marchetti, M., Vignoli, A., Balducci, D., Russo, L., Guerini, V., Barbui, T.: V617F JAK-2 mutation in patients with essential thrombocythemia: relation to platelet, granulocyte, and plasma hemostatic and inflammatory molecules. Exp. Hematol. **35**(5), 702–711 (2007)
38. Tilley, R.E., Holscher, T., Belani, R., Nieva, J., Mackman, N.: Tissue factor activity is increased in a combined platelet and microparticle sample from cancer patients. Thromb. Res. **122**(5), 604–609 (2008). S0049-3848(08)00003-0 [pii]10.1016/j.thromres.2007.12.023
39. Gerrits, A.J., Koekman, C.A., van Haeften, T.W., Akkerman, J.W.: Platelet tissue factor synthesis in type 2 diabetic patients is resistant to inhibition by insulin. Diabetes **59**(6), 1487–1495 (2010). db09-1008 [pii]10.2337/db09-1008
40. Watson, S.P., Bahou, W.F., Fitzgerald, D., Ouwehand, W., Rao, A.K., Leavitt, A.D.: Mapping the platelet proteome: a report of the ISTH platelet physiology subcommittee. J. Thromb. Haemost. **3**(9), 2098–2101 (2005). JTH1550 [pii]10.1111/j.1538-7836.2005.01550.x
41. Wang, L., Erling, P., Bengtsson, A.A., Truedsson, L., Sturfelt, G., Erlinge, D.: Transcriptional down-regulation of the platelet ADP receptor P2Y(12) and clusterin in patients with systemic lupus erythematosus. J. Thromb. Haemost. **2**(8), 1436–1442 (2004). 10.1111/j.1538-7836.2004.00854.x
42. Raghavachari, N., Xu, X., Harris, A., Villagra, J., Logun, C., Barb, J., Solomon, M.A., Suffredini, A.F., Danner, R.L., Kato, G., Munson, P.J., Morris Jr., S.M., Gladwin, M.T.: Amplified expression profiling of platelet transcriptome reveals changes in arginine metabolic pathways in patients with sickle cell disease. Circulation **115**(12), 1551–1562 (2007). 10.1161/ CIRCULATIONAHA.106.658641
43. Healy, A.M., Pickard, M.D., Pradhan, A.D., Wang, Y., Chen, Z., Croce, K., Sakuma, M., Shi, C., Zago, A.C., Garasic, J., Damokosh, A.I., Dowie, T.L., Poisson, L., Lillie, J., Libby, P., Ridker, P.M., Simon, D.I.: Platelet expression profiling and clinical validation of myeloid-related protein-14 as a novel determinant of cardiovascular events. Circulation **113**(19), 2278–2284 (2006). 10.1161/CIRCULATIONAHA.105.607333
44. Colombo, G., Gertow, K., Marenzi, G., Brambilla, M., De Metrio, M., Tremoli, E., Camera, M.: Gene expression profiling reveals multiple differences in platelets from patients with stable angina or non-ST elevation acute coronary syndrome. Thromb. Res. **128**(2), 161–168 (2011). 10.1016/j.thromres.2011.02.012
45. Wilkins, M.R., Sanchez, J.C., Gooley, A.A., Appel, R.D., Humphery-Smith, I., Hochstrasser, D.F., Williams, K.L.: Progress with proteome projects: why all proteins expressed by a genome should be identified and how to do it. Biotechnol. Genet. Eng. Rev. **13**, 19–50 (1996)
46. Shantsila, E., Kamphuisen, P.W., Lip, G.Y.: Circulating microparticles in cardiovascular disease: implications for atherogenesis and atherothrombosis. J. Thromb. Haemost. **8**(11), 2358–2368 (2010). JTH4007 [pii]10.1111/j.1538-7836.2010.04007.x
47. Barderas, M.G., Tunon, J., Darde, V.M., De la Cuesta, F., Duran, M.C., Jimenez-Nacher, J.J., Tarin, N., Lopez-Bescos, L., Egido, J., Vivanco, F.: Circulating human monocytes in the acute coronary syndrome express a characteristic proteomic profile. J. Proteome Res. **6**(2), 876–886 (2007). 10.1021/pr0601990
48. Banfi, C., Brioschi, M., Marenzi, G., De Metrio, M., Camera, M., Mussoni, L., Tremoli, E.: Proteome of platelets in patients with coronary artery disease. Exp. Hematol. **38**(5), 341–350 (2010). S0301-472X(10)00078-0 [pii]10.1016/j.exphem.2010.03.001

Printed in the United States
By Bookmasters

Printed in the United States
By Bookmasters